Fearless Flash

How to Use Adobe InDesign CS5 and the Tools You Already Know to Create Engaging Web Experiences

Claudia McCue

Fearless Flash

Claudia McCue

This Adobe Press book is published by Peachpit.

Peachpit
1249 Eighth Street
Berkeley, CA 94710
510/524-2178
510/524-2221 (fax)

Peachpit is a division of Pearson Education.
For the latest on Adobe Press books, go to www.adobepress.com
To report errors, please send a note to errata@peachpit.com

Copyright © 2011 by Claudia McCue

Project Editor: Susan Rimerman
Production Editor: Lisa Brazieal
Developmental/Copy Editor: Erfert Fenton
Technical Editor: Jean-Claude Tremblay
Proofreader: Scout Festa
Indexer: Karin Arrigoni
Cover Design: Aren Howell
Cover Illustration: Giovanni Meroni
Interior Design: Kathleen Cunningham

ISBN-13: 978-0-321-73482-2
ISBN-10:   0-321-73482-3

9 8 7 6 5 4 3 2 1

Printed and bound in the United States of America

For my North Star

Table of Contents

Introduction

More than once, I had sworn "I am going to learn how to use Adobe Flash." I had resolved to branch out from my lifelong print-centric comfort zone and get hip. So I'd crank up Flash, meditate on the interface that looked so little like my old friends Photoshop and Illustrator, and say to myself, "I think I'll go do some laundry."

I secretly envied designers who could make their content wiggle and bark, and dreamed that someday I'd be able to do that, too. But, frankly, Flash intimidated me.

Then along came Adobe InDesign CS5, with a hefty arsenal of new interactive tools, accompanied by the new Adobe Flash Catalyst CS5—both refreshingly code-free.

Suddenly, there was hope.

Who Should Read This Book

If you're a print designer who has memorized most of the Pantone color numbers but has no idea what hexadecimal color codes are, being able to use familiar tools to create interactive content would be a new lease on your professional life. If you're feeling a bit obsolete when you see coders whip out onscreen magic, don't give up. You *don't* have to completely retrain your brain.

As a print designer, you've accumulated years of design savvy, honed your visual instincts, and practiced your production chops. And not a minute of that experience will be wasted when you begin designing pages for the Web. You don't have to start over; you can hit the ground running, because you already know how to use the foundation tools in InDesign, Photoshop, and Illustrator. And even though you've never used it, you'll find the Flash Catalyst interface friendly and intuitive.

Instead of having to switch gears completely, you can build on what you already know, and apply your capabilities to interactive projects. This book can get you off to a good start on your new adventure.

What You'll Get Out of This Book

While there isn't room in this book to walk you through every single feature in InDesign, Photoshop, Illustrator, Flash Catalyst, and Flash Professional, you'll pick up valuable new techniques for adding interactivity, including:

- Awakening InDesign's secret built-in Animation Encyclopedia
- Animating InDesign page content with motion presets
- Controlling the speed and play order of animations
- Creating and applying custom motion presets
- Creating custom button artwork in Photoshop, Illustrator, and InDesign
- Importing video content and controlling poster and player options
- Exporting to Flash Professional (and learning what's lost in translation)
- Editing animations in Flash Professional
- Using the intuitive Heads Up Display in Flash Catalyst to turn Illustrator and Photoshop documents into interactive projects
- Refining your files for online, in-house, or disc deployment

And you'll do all of this without writing a single line of code!

What I hope you get out of this book is a sense of relief *(This isn't so hard after all!)* and a bit of inspiration *(This is actually fun!)*.

What This Book is *Not*

This book doesn't presume to teach you design principles. I'm a mechanic, not a designer. *You're* the designer. All I can provide is insight into the inner workings of these tools. I'm counting on you to make it look good!

This is not a programming book. It's devoted to helping you *avoid* writing code. But don't let that scare you away from the more technical possibilities. Mere mortals *can* learn ActionScript and make Flash Professional sing. I've written JavaScript to enhance Adobe Acrobat forms, and I am definitely not a programmer. It may be that this book will whet your appetite and inspire you to dig deeper into what you used to think were foreign territories. That would make me proud.

Software Requirements

Unless you're planning on just reading this book at the beach (unlikely), you'll need all the appropriate software to play along. The following Adobe applications are used in the exercises:

- InDesign CS5
- Photoshop CS5
- Illustrator CS5
- Flash Catalyst CS5
- Flash Professional CS5

If you have Adobe Creative Suite 5 Design Premium or Adobe Creative Suite 5 Master Collection, you have all the necessary software.

As for hardware requirements, as long as you have sufficient horsepower to run the required software, you're fully equipped. It wouldn't hurt to have sufficient RAM that you can run several applications simultaneously, and there's no such thing as too much hard drive space. See www.adobe.com/products/creativesuite for official system requirements.

If you have your own Web site, you'll be able to upload finished project files and test them. If not, you can test them on your own computer.

About the Exercise Files

The exercise files used in this book are organized by chapter on the CD. You can copy them all to your hard drive before you start working, or copy the exercise files for each chapter as needed. (Note: There are no exercise files for Chapter 6.) Because you will be working on and saving components of projects, then combining those components into finished work, it will be easier (and saner) to work off your local hard drive rather than trying to work off the CD. Most of the exercises include final versions of the working files and final exported SWF files so you can check your work. There is no homework, and there are no tests (unless you count your boss asking, "Hey, since I gave you that book yesterday, can you have that interactive portfolio ready in the morning?").

All fonts required by the exercises are installed with Creative Suite 5, so you should not encounter any "missing font" messages unless you've manually modified your repository of fonts.

While you're welcome to rework and experiment with any content in the exercises, please don't use any of the images or artwork commercially.

Acknowledgments

When I first saw the interactive features in InDesign CS5 and met the new kid on the block, Flash Catalyst, I was smitten. I thought, "I should write a book." So I have to thank the gifted Adobe software wizards who somehow manage to think up compelling new features with every release. I'm convinced they have access to alien technology. (Have you seen Content Aware Fill in Photoshop CS5? I rest my case.)

My thanks to Susan Rimerman for thinking this book might be a good idea, and for exercising industrial-strength patience. It was a treat to work once again with Lisa Brazieal as production editor. Jean-Claude Tremblay was invaluable as an eagle-eyed technical editor, and offered indispensable insight into Flash Professional. I owe him something a bit more tangible than gratitude. (I only hope he doesn't say, "Oh, a Lamborghini will do.") And while being edited might be an unconventional way to gain a new friend, that's what happened as a result of having the delightful Erfert Fenton as an editor. I hope to actually meet all these people someday.

Chapter 1

Meet Your New Toys

If you've been using Adobe InDesign to create pages for print, you're probably comfortable with InDesign's interface and way of thinking. So don't be hesitant about branching out into the new interactive features of InDesign CS5; theyll feel immediately familiar to you even if you've never used any other tool to create animation or interactive content. That's the whole idea!

Think of this chapter as a sort of warm-up lap to introduce you to the new tools you'll be using. As you explore the new panels and features, you'll add animation and interactive elements to a lesson file and discover how painless (and fun) it can be. You'll learn how to apply and modify motion animation to make a headline drop gracefully into a page, how to import and play video, and how to preview your work before exporting. You'll even make a slideshow from simple graphic frames.

In later chapters, you'll go into more depth with the tools you meet in this one, and before you know it you'll be a whiz at bringing pages to life!

Before you venture into the brave new world of interactivity, it's helpful to know the meaning of a couple of important acronyms. Here's your decoder ring:

FLA: The native format of Adobe Flash Professional. FLA files can be edited in Flash Professional, but can't be viewed online. Think of FLA files as the working format for Flash; they must be exported to the SWF format for viewing.

SWF: The letters stand for ShockWave Flash, the origins of which go back to a product called FutureSplash Animator, which was a competitor to Macromedia's Shockwave. When FutureSplash was acquired by Macromedia, its name was truncated to Flash. Flash forward (so to speak) to 2005, and Flash becomes an Adobe product. The SWF format can be viewed in Adobe Flash Player (formerly the Adobe Shockwave Player), but cannot be edited in Flash. SWF files can include hyperlinks, animations, movies, sounds, page transitions, and buttons.

InDesign CS5 can export FLA (editable Flash) files, which can then be further edited in Adobe Flash Professional. You'll discover, though, that some of the behaviors created in InDesign can only be replicated or modified in Flash Professional by using a Flash-specific programming language called *ActionScript.* ActionScript allows you to manipulate objects and the Flash timeline to control behavior and interactions with objects. If you wish to go beyond the Flash capabilities of InDesign CS5, you'll need to dedicate time to learning Flash and ActionScript. While ActionScript is beyond the scope of this book, I'll recommend some resources later for those who want to dig deeper.

InDesign CS5 can also export SWF files, which can be viewed online and placed into other InDesign files or Adobe PDFs, but can't be modified in Flash. However, SWF files can be imported into a Flash project as components.

Since this book is largely focused on the Flash creation features of InDesign CS5, we'll concentrate mainly on the tools for Flash content. But we'll also explore the additions to the PDF creation options so you'll be comfortable regardless of the export format you choose. As you'll discover, while there is some overlap between the capabilities of the SWF format and those of interactive Adobe Acrobat PDFs, Flash/SWF features are richer and more flexible than those supported by interactive PDFs alone. I'll discuss the differences between SWF and interactive PDF capabilities later in this book.

Let's Go Exploring

It's time to explore InDesign's new interactive panels. They're easy to spot. Choose one of the new workspaces—Interactive or Interactive for PDF—and there they are (**Figures 1.1** and **1.2**).

Figure 1.1 (left) Choose the new Interactive workspace to see panels appropriate for creating Flash content.

Figure 1.2 (right) Choose the new Interactive for PDF workspace to activate panels appropriate for creating interactive PDFs.

The new additions are Animation, Media, Object States, Preview, and Timing. (Bookmarks, Buttons, Hyperlinks, and Page Transitions are not new to InDesign CS5.) To access panels that govern interactive functions, choose Window > Interactive; all the necessary panels are available through a submenu.

Now we'll take a look at the new panels that create and control interactive features; we'll explore all the interactive panels (old and new) in later chapters.

Animation Panel

NOTE: Initially, the Animation panel does not display the Properties controls. Click the small triangle to the left of the Properties label to reveal the bottom half of the Animation panel. You'll want access to the Properties controls frequently, so this may be your preferred mode for the Animation panel.

Using the controls in the Animation panel, you can name a target object something meaningful (rather than just "rectangle" or the filename of a graphic), apply one of the many motion presets, specify when the animation is triggered and how it will play, scale the object over the course of the animation, and even control its opacity. Any object in an InDesign document can be animated; you can create flying text frames, graphics that slowly become fully opaque, even objects that twirl around.

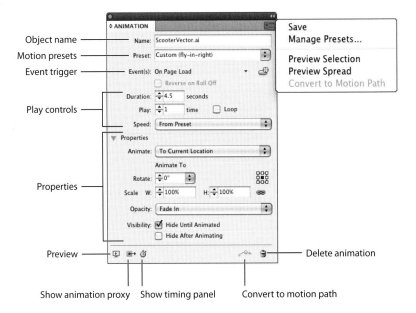

Object Name If an object is a frame containing a placed graphic, it's initially identified in the revamped Layers panel by the filename of the graphic. But you can change this to something more meaningful by renaming the object in the Layers panel or the Animation panel. Because you might use a button or other trigger to activate the animation of this object, you should give it a name you'll remember later. And if you plan to place a graphic several times in a spread, but want to have each instance do something different, each frame will need its own unique name.

Now you'll explore the important sections of the Animation panel by adding some animation to an object in a project. To get started, copy the **Ch_1_Exercise** folder to your hard drive.

Motion Presets In this exercise, you'll use the Animation panel to make a headline drop in from the top of the screen. The headline starts life as a simple bit of Adobe Illustrator artwork, but you're going to make it fly!

1. Launch InDesign CS5, and open the file **VintageAd_start.indd**. If you can't see any of the pasteboard above the page, zoom out a bit.

2. Choose File > Save As, and save the file as **VintageAd_working.indd**.

3. Choose the Interactive workspace; you can choose Window > Workspace > Interactive, or choose from the Workspace pull-down menu near the right side of the Control panel.

4. Click the Animation panel button to expand the panel. Click the triangle next to the Properties control at the bottom of the panel to reveal all the options.

5. Choose the Selection tool (hereinafter referred to by its common name, "black arrow"), and select the **Vintage Motocross** headline. Note that in the Animation panel it's identified by the artwork filename **VintageHeader.ai**.

6. In the Animation panel, change the name of the object to **Headline**, and then choose the Fly in from Top motion preset. The Animation panel shows a quick preview at the top, giving you an idea of what the motion preset does; a purple butterfly (a nod to InDesign's original icon/mascot) drifts gracefully down from the top of the panel. Notice the green animation line that appears above the headline artwork in the document page; this represents the start and end points for the fly-in motion.

7. You can preview the results of the animation settings by clicking the small Preview icon () at the lower-left corner of the Animation panel; you should see the headline fly in from the top (**Figure 1.3**). You can pull on the corners of the Preview window to make it larger.

TIP: The animation line is a Bézier path, which means that you can edit its shape with the Pen tool. If you want to experiment, just select the animation line with the Direct Selection tool (white arrow), then switch to the Pen tool to add curvature. Whee!

Figure 1.3 Test your animation in the Preview panel. You can also launch Preview from the Animation, Timing, and Buttons panels.

8. If you want to change the speed of the headline's fly-in, experiment with the Duration settings in the Play Controls section of the Animation panel. You can even loop the fly-in (but that's a cruel thing to do to the end user).

Event Trigger By default, animations play automatically when the page is displayed, but animations can be triggered by other events, such as the click of a button. In the **Vintage Motocross** file, there is a custom animation already in place, but it doesn't yet have any trigger to set it in motion. You'll fix the animation so it's triggered when the page is displayed.

1. In the Layers panel, click the eyeball visibility control to show the **wheel** layer, and then click the triangle to the left of the layer name to expand the display of the layer's contents. There's only one object in the layer, an Illustrator file named **BikeWheel.ai**. Click the small square to the right of the **BikeWheel.ai** entry in the layer to target the bike wheel artwork. If necessary, zoom out to see the wheel artwork in the pasteboard to the right of the page.

2. Select the wheel with the black arrow, and you'll see the curving green line that indicates a custom motion preset (**Figure 1.4**). In a later exercise, you'll create your own custom motion preset; any path can become a motion guide for an animation.

Figure 1.4 Select the wheel art to view the custom motion path.

3. In the Animation panel, note that the preset is labeled as Custom, but there's no event listed as a trigger to start the animation. Click the small downward-pointing triangle next to the word **Choose** to select On Page Load from the pull-down menu that appears (**Figure 1.5**). Set the Duration to 3.5 seconds.

Figure 1.5 Choose On Page Load to trigger the wheel animation. Note the other options available.

4. Click the Preview icon at the bottom left of the Animation panel to open the Preview panel and see the results. Note how the wheel follows the curving motion path.

5. Save the file, and keep it open for the next section.

Play Controls While the canned motion presets are a great start, you'll often want to modify the behavior of an animation. You can control the duration, repetition, and pace of the animation with the play controls in the Animation panel.

1. If necessary, reselect the wheel and open the Animation panel. If the Properties section of the panel is hidden, click the triangle to the left of the Properties control to display the additional controls.

2. Change the Speed setting to Ease Out and preview the result. Notice how the wheel slows down before it comes to a stop, rather than moving at a uniform speed.

3. Change the Rotate attribute to -180°—now the wheel will spin slowly during its animation. Change the Duration to 5 seconds, and preview the result.

4. Set the Opacity to Fade In and preview the change.

5. Change the Opacity back to None (meaning that there will be no opacity effects), and then change the Scale setting to 50% and preview the results. The wheel looks like it's bouncing away from you as it moves from right to left.

6. Save the file, and leave it open for the next section.

Preview Panel

As you add more complexity to interactive documents, you may wish to concentrate on the behavior of a single object, or test links that jump to other spreads in the file, or hyperlinks that lead to Web sites. By default, the Preview

TIP: Pull the Preview panel loose from the panel dock so that it's a floating panel, and pull on its corners to increase its size. That way, every time you choose to preview by clicking the Preview icon in the Animation, Timing, or Buttons panel, you can keep the original panel open while previewing.

panel shows the current spread, but you can change that. It also offers navigation controls, allowing you to page through a multipage document to test internal links. In addition, the Preview panel warns you if links are missing, or if any content is incompatible with the Flash Player (**Figure 1.6**).

Figure 1.6 Preview panel controls and options

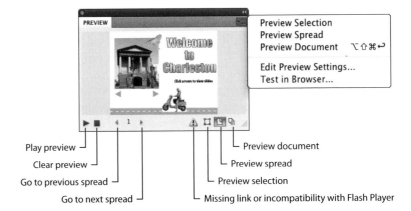

1. Select the wheel, and choose the Preview Selection option (⬚) and click the Play button (▶) in the Preview panel. Only the wheel animation appears in the Preview panel.

2. With the wheel still selected, choose the Preview Spread option (▣) and click the Play button again to see the entire page in action. Since this document has only one single-page spread, the Preview Document button (▣) won't be helpful. (Although it might seem odd to refer to a single page as a spread, that's how InDesign thinks of a single, non-facing page. You can have from one to ten pages in a spread. If you wish to view the behavior of the entire document—for example, to test cross-references—the Preview Document option is very helpful.)

3. Keep the document open for the next section.

Timing Panel

Animations play in the order in which they were created, which is not always what you want. You may want to change the order of animations, or have multiple animations play simultaneously. The Timing panel (**Figure 1.7**) helps you control the order in which animations play, and gives you the option of setting a delay between a triggering event and the beginning of an animation.

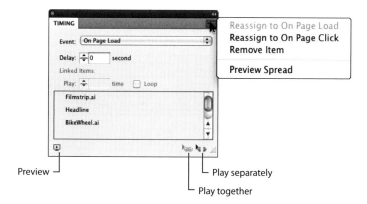

Preview

Play separately

Play together

Figure 1.7 The Timing panel lets you control the order of animations, as well as add delays. You can set multiple animations to play simultaneously.

1. In the Layers panel, click the visibility control for the **video** layer, and then click the triangle to the left of the layer name to display the objects in the layer. The only object is the filmstrip artwork, **Filmstrip.ai**. Click the small square to the right of the Filmstrip.ai name to target it. Because the filmstrip art is the only object in the video layer, you can also Option-click or Alt-click the layer name; this selects all objects in a layer. The black filmstrip art looks static, but it is set to fade in slowly.

2. Preview the animation by clicking the Play button in the Preview panel, or by clicking the Preview icon in the Timing panel. Notice that the filmstrip fades in before the headline and wheel animations occur. You'll change that in the following steps.

3. Select the filmstrip art and look at its behavior in the Animation panel; it's set to use the Fade-in preset, with a custom duration of 1 second.

4. Open the **Timing** panel (Window > Interactive > Timing). The **Filmstrip.ai** art is first in the list, so it plays before the headline and wheel animations start. Change the order of animations by dragging the **Filmstrip.ai** object to the bottom of the list (**Figure 1.8**). Now it will play after the headline drop and wheel-roll are finished. Test the results by clicking the Preview icon in the Timing panel.

5. You've corrected the order in which the animations play, but now there's an awkward delay before the filmstrip art appears. In the Timing panel, select the **BikeWheel.ai** object, and then Shift-click the **Filmstrip.ai** object. Click the **Play Together** icon () at the bottom of the Timing panel. Preview the new timing; now the filmstrip fades in as the wheel rolls, but its appearance covers up the last bit of the wheel's trip across the page.

Figure 1.8 Change the order of animations by dragging the **Filmstrip.ai** object to the bottom of the list in the Timing panel.

6. If you play the filmstrip after the wheel, it's too late. If you play the filmstrip simultaneously with the wheel, it's too early. What's the "just right" solution? Add a little delay to the filmstrip's appearance. Select the Filmstrip.ai object in the Timing panel, and set the Delay to 1.75 seconds (you can use the up/down controls to the left of the Delay field rather than bothering with typing).

7. Preview the new setting and see what you think. The filmstrip fades in just as the wheel disappears behind it. While it might seem counterintuitive to play two animations simultaneously while adding a delay to one of them, sometimes it's the easiest way to exercise granular control over what plays when. Save the file and leave it open for the next section.

Media Panel

InDesign CS5 allows you to import high-quality video and audio, and makes it easy to add professional-looking play controls. The Media panel (**Figure 1.9**) gives you control over the appearance and behavior of multimedia files.

Figure 1.9 Use the Media panel to control the behavior of placed audio and video files. You can even add navigation points to a video, which can be triggered by buttons or events.

As with animations, you can control what triggers the multimedia content to play. You can also add a *poster* to represent the multimedia in the page if you want to control its appearance. A poster can be a frame from the video, a high-resolution image to represent an audio or video file, or InDesign's default graphic placeholders.

1. In the **VintageAd_working.indd** file, target the **video** layer. You'll place a video on top of the filmstrip art. Choose File > Place, navigate to the **Ch_1_Exercise** folder, and select **moto1.f4v**. Click in the page to place the file on the filmstrip art. Select the video with the black arrow and, using the mouse or your keyboard arrows, position the outline of the video so it looks like a frame in the filmstrip (**Figure 1.10**).

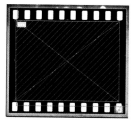

Figure 1.10 A placed video initially just indicates the area occupied by the file. The green frame and stripes do not print or appear in exported files.

2. Now you'll experiment with the four options InDesign offers for the representation of the video in the document. If necessary, select the placed video with the black arrow, and choose the None option in the Poster pull-down menu in the Media panel. To see how the video will appear in the final export, press Command-Shift-Return (Macintosh) or Ctrl-Shift-Enter (Windows) to open the Preview panel and run the animation. Because (oddly) there is no option in the Media panel to automatically launch Preview, the keystroke-combo method is easier than accessing the Preview panel manually. The green outline and diagonal lines disappear, and there's no indication that a video exists in that location. To play the video, the end user would have to accidentally click the video's location, or you'd have to provide some other guidance (such as a caption or a clickable button that plays the video). There's such a thing as being too subtle; you need to help the end user find content and interactive features if they're not obvious.

Figure 1.11 The Standard poster displays a white rectangle containing a filmstrip icon.

3. InDesign offers built-in generic filmstrip artwork to represent a video. If necessary, reselect the video, and then choose the Standard option from the Poster pull-down menu in the Media panel. Press Command-Shift-Return (Macintosh) or Ctrl-Shift-Enter (Windows) to open the Preview panel and run the animation. As before, the green frame and diagonal lines disappear because they're just indicators of the area of the video (**Figure 1.11**). If you didn't have the cute Illustrator filmstrip artwork, the Standard option might be OK, but there are more attractive options.

Figure 1.12 The Current Frame represents the video with a frame you choose from the video.

4. If necessary, select the placed video with the black arrow, and then choose the From Current Frame option in the Poster pull-down menu in the Media panel. By default, InDesign displays the first frame of the video, but you can select any frame. You can drag the little slider underneath the preview pane in the Media panel to find a frame you like, or you can step back and forth through the frames one by one by using the left and right arrow keys on your keyboard. There's a nice frame at the 00:06.63 mark

Figure 1.13 You can represent the video with any image. Here, the image also acts as a hint that there's a video in the document.

(**Figure 1.12**). To designate the chosen frame as the poster, click the pair of curly arrows to the right of the From Current Frame pull-down menu. To see how the video will appear in the final export, press Command-Shift-Return (Macintosh) or Ctrl-Shift-Enter (Windows) to open the Preview panel and run the animation.

5. If you want a different image to represent the video in the document, you can choose any PSD, TIFF, PNG, JPEG, or GIF image for placement (you can't use Illustrator AI or EPS files, though). When you place the image, you can then reposition and scale it as you would any image. It will seem as though you actually have two items occupying the same frame in the document: the video, and the image representing it.

If necessary, reselect the placed video with the black arrow, and select the Choose Image option in the Poster pull-down menu in the Media panel. Navigate to the **Ch_1_Exercise** folder and select **MoviePoster.psd**. If necessary, choose Object > Fitting > Fill Frame Proportionally (**Figure 1.13**). Play the preview to check the results. The new poster lets the viewer know they should click to play the video; however, if they click immediately they might miss the descending headline and bouncing wheel. Instead, it would be nice if the image faded in after the headline, wheel, and filmstrip art.

6. Look in the Animation, Media, and Timing panels; there's no way to address the speed or timing of the appearance of the poster image, since it's more or less considered a decoration for the video. So you'll have to cheat. Since a poster can't be animated, you'll remove it from the video. Select the frame containing the video and poster and choose the None poster option in the Media panel.

7. Choose File > Place, and then choose **MoviePoster.psd**. Now you're placing it as a graphic, not as a poster attribute for the video, so you can handle it a bit differently. Position it appropriately on top of the filmstrip art. It should fit nicely, since its size was set to match the pixel dimensions of the video, but of course that's not necessary. In the Layers panel, drag the **MoviePoster.psd** object below the **moto1.f4v** video object (**Figure 1.14**); otherwise, the video won't be clickable. Keep the poster frame selected for the next step.

Figure 1.14 Make sure the video is above the poster in stacking order, or it won't be selectable or clickable.

8. In the Animation panel, choose the Fade-In preset, and leave the other settings at their defaults. Look in the Timing panel: The poster image fades in last because it's last in the list of animations. The default timing works nicely, but you can modify it if you like. Press Command-Shift-Return (Macintosh) or Ctrl-Shift-Enter (Windows) to open the Preview panel and run the animation.

9. It would be nice to add a play controller to the video so the end user can play, pause, and stop the video. InDesign provides a number of prebuilt controller skins for you to use. In the Layers panel, click the small triangle to the left of the name of the video layer to display all the objects in the layer. Target the video by clicking the small green square to the right of the video's name, <**moto1.f4v**> (or just select the video in the document with the black arrow). In the Media panel, choose SkinOverAllNoCaption from the Controller pull-down menu, and select the Show Controller on Rollover option (**Figure 1.15**). (The rollover option causes the controller to appear when the user mouses over a running video; it does not cause the controller to appear if the user mouses over the area of the video before the video has been triggered to run.)

TIP: You can name any object in the Layers panel. By default, geometric shapes are named by their species (rectangle, ellipse, etc.), and placed graphics are named by their filename, but you can modify the name of any object. Just select the object in the Layers panel, wait a second, and the name will highlight for retyping. This can help you retain your sanity in a very complex document.

Figure 1.15 InDesign offers an extensive selection of controller skins that allow the end user to play, pause, and stop the video.

You can embed video for viewing in a SWF or interactive PDF, or you can include external links that refer to the video file. While external links mean that you don't have to host (or include) the video file, this method can complicate deployment if the target video is moved or deleted.

While InDesign allows you to place a number of multimedia formats, the appropriate format for your project depends on how you plan to export it, and the capabilities of your proposed audience.

While you can place multimedia files in Flash Video (FLV, F4V), H.264-encoded files (for example, MP4), QuickTime (MOV), AVI or SWF format, only certain types (FLV, F4V, SWF, MP3, MP4) are supported by Adobe Flash Player version 10 or later.

QuickTime (MOV), AVI, and MPEG are supported in exported interactive PDFs, but not in exported Flash (SWF or FLA) files.

For maximum flexibility, stick with the FLV and F4V formats for video, and the MP3 format for audio, and educate your potential audience so they can take advantage of rich media. Gently suggest (or insist) that they adopt the most recent version of Adobe Flash Player. Provide links for the current download for the free Flash Player.

Object States

Multistate objects consist of groups of multiple frames linked together by a common behavior; their appearance can be triggered by external sources, such as buttons. One of the most common uses for multistate objects is to create slideshows. The Object States panel (**Figure 1.16**) allows you to add or delete states, and to control the visibility of the multistate object until it is triggered.

Figure 1.16 Multistate objects consist of multiple frames that are all governed by an external trigger, such as a button.

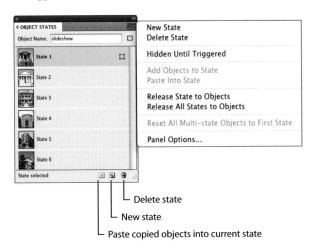

1. You'll convert several graphic frames into a single multistate object, which will be controlled by two clickable buttons. In the Layers panel, select the **slideshow** layer and click the small triangle to the left of the layer name to reveal all the objects in the layer. Click the small square to the right of the object named <**moto_1.jpg**>. Holding down the Shift key, click <**moto_2.jpg**>, <**moto_3.jpg**>, and <**moto_4.jpg**>. Alternatively, since the moto images are the only objects in the slideshow layer, you can Option/Alt-click the small square to the right of the slideshow layer name in the Layers panel.

2. Using either the Align controls in the Control panel or the Align panel (Window > Object & Layout > Align), align the top and left edges of the four selected frames (**Figure 1.17**). You don't need to group the objects; just keep them selected for the next step.

Figure 1.17 Shift-click to target and select the four moto images in the Layers panel (left), and then align their top and left edges (below).

3. In the Object States panel (Window > Interactive > Object States), click the Convert Selection to Multistate Object button ( ) at the bottom of the panel. Name the new multistate object **motoslides**.

4. Now you'll set up the yellow triangle buttons to page through the slideshow created by the multistate object. (Later in the book, you'll learn how to create and control buttons. In this document, you've been given a head start; the buttons are already in place, and you'll just have to add the appropriate actions.) Select the left triangle, and then open the Buttons panel (Window > Interactive > Buttons). Name the button **prev**, and then click the small plus sign to the right of the word Actions. Choose Go to Previous State from the pull-down menu. The Object pull-down should automatically read **motoslides**, since it's the only multistate object in the document.

5. Select the right yellow triangle and then follow the steps above, but assign the Go to Next State action. By default, the slideshow will cycle when the end user clicks the buttons; you can restrict this by checking the Stop at First State option. For this document, leave that option unchecked. See **Figure 1.18** for the correct settings.

Figure 1.18 Use these settings for the triangle buttons that will allow the end user to cycle through the slideshow.

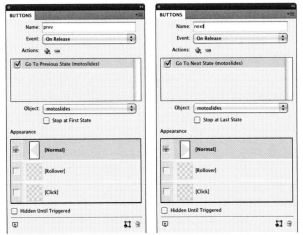

6. Reselect the **motoslides** multistate object if necessary, and then Shift-click to select the two triangular buttons on either side of the slides. Group all three objects together, and then preview the results; you can test the buttons in the Preview panel. (It's not necessary to group the objects for functionality; the buttons will recognize their target by object name whether they're grouped or not. But grouping ensures that the arrangement of objects will be maintained if you click accidentally. Additionally, if the entire slideshow-and-button assembly is grouped, you could add animation to the whole shebang at a later time.)

7. Now—finally!—you'll export your project and view it in a browser. Save your working file, and then choose File > Save As and name the file **VintageAd_final.indd**. Create a folder (say, on your desktop), then return to InDesign and choose File > Export, choosing Flash Player (SWF) for the export format. Make sure the default View SWF After Exporting option is checked, leave everything at the defaults, and click OK. Your default browser should launch, and you can test all the features you've created. You'll see the headline descend, and the wheel bounce in from the right. Play the video, experimenting with the controller. Cycle through the slideshow, making sure the buttons work as you expect.

Isn't that cool? And you didn't have to write a single line of code!

8. Open the folder you created, and view the directory structure and files that were created as you worked on your project (**Figure 1.19**). InDesign creates a "host" HTML file to contain and display the SWF in a browser; if you're curious, open the HTML file in a text editor to see what's inside. It may look foreign if you've never looked at HTML code before, but it makes sense to a developer who might build on this basic start (or start from scratch). The entire folder should take up less than 1.5MB of disk space.

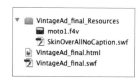

Figure 1.19 View the files that were created when you exported the project to SWF.

Looking Ahead

In future chapters, we'll dig deeper into the functions of the interactive tools; the more you know, the more fun you can have. It's also important to consider the end user's experience. For truly successful deployment of your interactive content, you have to anticipate the user's needs and reactions to your interactive documents. This can mean a lot of hard work on your part in order to make it much easier for the person on the other side of the screen. Later on, we'll tackle best practices and deployment issues to get you headed in the right direction.

Chapter 2

Basic Interactivity and Navigation

Designing for onscreen viewing is a bit different from designing for print. It's not just a matter of switching to a horizontal format; you have to simplify presentation and help the end user find a logical path through the content. As the content creator, you have to work really hard to make things very easy for the user. You have to anticipate the user's needs to ensure that their experience is positive. While the goal is still to present information in an attractive way, the approach has to be a bit different in terms of presentation, navigation, and deployment.

Presentation

The readers of a printed piece are viewing content by reflected light; if text is hard to read, they can seek a brighter reading light (or stronger glasses). But the viewer of onscreen content has limited options; they're unlikely to fiddle with the monitor resolution or brightness to read small or illegible text. It's up to you to anticipate the user's viewing conditions and compensate for the realities of onscreen viewing.

View a PDF of a printed piece onscreen, and you'll start to get an idea of some of the differences between printed and onscreen documents. Open the file **BF_Print.pdf** in the **Ch_2_Exercise** folder (**Figure 2.1**).

Figure 2.1 A four-page brochure that's appropriate for print needs to be reformatted horizontally for effective onscreen viewing.

Start thinking about what you'd change if you were repurposing this content for a better onscreen viewing experience. Whether you're planning to create Flash, PDF, or HTML content, the issues are largely the same. Here are some considerations:

- **Use a horizontal format.** This is perhaps the most obvious difference between print and onscreen viewing. Most print materials follow a vertical format, which doesn't always translate comfortably to the horizontal format of computer monitors. Plan your design with the horizontal format in mind; it will dictate your layout as well as your choice of content. For example, landscape-format images may fit into your design more easily than tall, narrow graphics (see **Figure 2.2**).

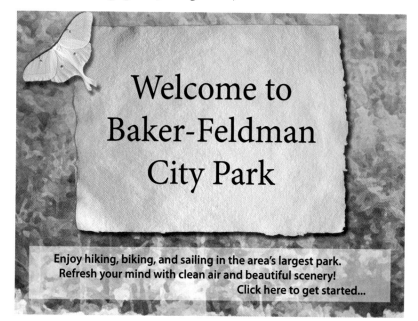

Figure 2.2 The same content, formatted for onscreen viewing. Note the larger graphics, simpler text, and horizontal page format.

- **Use a screen-appropriate page size.** Just switching a letter-sized or A4 page to landscape mode isn't quite the answer. Even though most users have a reasonably sized monitor that's capable of at least 1024 by 768 resolution (and many have monitors capable of even higher resolutions), filling the entire area of that screen isn't necessary (or optimal). InDesign offers several default document presets that are appropriate for Web-based viewing.

- **Shorten the line length of text.** Readers are more comfortable with shorter line lengths (3 to 6 inches), even when reading printed content. Do a little experiment: Open a few magazines and books, and take note of your own reading experience. You'll find that when you're traversing longer lines, you use a few extra microseconds to find the start of the next line. Shorter line widths yield easier reading. Of course, this can require more vertical scrolling or multipage navigation if you have lots of text. This leads to the next point...

- **Simplify editorial content.** Unless you're being paid by the word, figure out a way to say more with less. Write more concisely. Replace a long paragraph with a well-crafted bullet point. Let headlines do some of the talking. Move secondary content to another location, and provide links for readers who want to dig deeper.

- **Ensure readability with legible text.** Minimum text size should be 10 or 12 points. While serif and sans serif fonts are equally readable at larger sizes, sans serif fonts are more reliable at smaller sizes, especially when text is white or light-colored on a dark background. Text size and styles aren't the only issues; contrast and color also play a part. Charcoal gray text on a black background may look chic in a printed piece, but onscreen viewing benefits from higher contrast. Red text on a green background is, well, just plain cruel.

- **Link to a printable version.** If you feel it's necessary to provide the reader with a print-oriented version (for example, to include a larger, more detailed map), include a link to a downloadable PDF.

Navigation

Readers don't need to be educated about how to read a book. When reading a novel, they know to start at the front cover and proceed toward the back (and the surprise ending). In a reference book, the table of contents is the primary navigational aid. For a reader thumbing through a book, chapter titles may be enough guidance. Rarely does a book consist of one long, uninterrupted flow of text; there are logical divisions to the content. In an online environment, you have to lead the viewer through your information so they follow a logical path. And you have to provide a clear method of navigating nonlinear content so they can find what's important. A SWF or interactive PDF file launches somewhat like a book, but the reader can't just thumb through it to get an aerial view. It's up to you to provide a road map. Think about some of the options:

Use a hyperlinked table of contents. A table of contents (TOC) doesn't have to be formal, with extensive descriptions and page numbers. Think of the TOC as the 10,000-foot view, giving the reader an idea where the major topics are to be found. Hyperlinked entries let the reader jump to the subject that interests them, without having to wade through other topics first. InDesign can generate a table of contents based on paragraph styles used in the document, and the TOC is automatically hyperlinked to the content it references, whether you export to SWF or interactive PDF. Bonus: Clickable bookmarks are generated from TOC entries in an interactive PDF.

Use cross-references. If portions of the content are interrelated, provide cross-references to enable the reader to quickly jump to related sections. InDesign CS5 makes this fairly easy, allowing you to create dynamic links based on text anchors or text tagged with paragraph styles.

Create hyperlinks. You can manually create hyperlinks to content within the same document (similar to cross-references, above) or to Web addresses that provide additional information. You can also use the hyperlink format to provide e-mail links for your readers.

Provide navigational aids. If a document is just a single run of text continued across multiple pages, it may be obvious to the reader that when they're finished reading the content of one page, they should go to the next page. But how do they get there? The page curl page-turning effect included in InDesign's default SWF export options is cute, but unless the user already knows that the corners of the page are "hot spots" that provide a mechanism for turning pages, he's doomed to stare at the same page forever. Help the reader by providing unambiguous controls, such as previous page/next page buttons, and a "home" button to take them back to a comfortable starting point, such as the first page or the table of contents.

Test your document. You've been looking at your project for so long that you don't have to think about the content or its presentation, so perhaps you're not the best judge of whether it's intuitive to navigate. Enlist an innocent bystander to test the navigability of the document. Do they need to be told what to click? Do they immediately understand the controls? If not, perhaps you need to make the controls simpler and more obvious, or provide an introductory page that explains the document's structure and navigational controls. If possible, choose a control subject who's typical of your potential audience; don't expect your Aunt Ruth to make sense of a highly stylized presentation intended for your design peers. (Although chances are if she can find her way around, almost anyone can. No offense to Aunt Ruth.)

Deployment

Once you've finished your interactive creation, the next step is to get it out into the world so other people can appreciate it. When content creation and testing are finished, it's time to export to SWF or interactive PDF. (Since this book is about Flash content, we'll limit this discussion to the SWF file format.)

You have several options for deploying SWF files:

- Post the file on the Web and provide the URL so users can view it in a Web browser (if they have Adobe Flash Player installed).

- Send the SWF on disc or as an email attachment and instruct the recipient to download and install the latest Flash Player (http://get.adobe.com/flashplayer). The user can then launch a browser and view the locally stored SWF file.

- Send the SWF file to users with Adobe Media Player (http://www.adobe.com/products/mediaplayer); they can open and play the SWF directly in Media Player.

- Embed the SWF file into a PDF and send the PDF to users with Adobe Acrobat 9 Standard or Adobe Acrobat 9 Pro, or Adobe Reader 9. While users of version 6.0 of Acrobat Standard, Pro, or Reader can view embedded video content, they must have the appropriate multimedia viewer installed (such as QuickTime or Windows Media Player). A multimedia viewer is built into Reader and Acrobat 9, so no external player is required. You can embed a SWF file in a PDF by opening the PDF in Acrobat 9 Pro and using Acrobat's multimedia tools. Alternatively, you can place the SWF into an InDesign CS5 document and export to interactive PDF. In either case, the PDF must have Acrobat 6 (PDF 1.5) or higher compatibility; support for embedded video and Flash content was introduced with Acrobat 6.0. (While earlier versions of InDesign allow the placement of SWF content, you may find that the SWF does not play correctly in the exported PDF. So stick with InDesign CS5 for best results.)

Adding Navigational Controls

Now you'll open a file in progress and add cross-references and navigation buttons to help the end user get around. You'll also create a Table of Contents style so InDesign can generate an automatically hyperlinked table of contents. You'll create a rollover effect that allows the user to display additional content. And you'll be pleasantly surprised at how easy all of this is.

To view the final version of the project, launch a Web browser with the current version of Adobe Flash Player installed, navigate to the **Finished** folder inside the **Ch_2_Exercise** folder, and open **index.html**. (If you're using Adobe Media Player, just open the SWF file in that folder, **bfpark.swf**.) Page through the document, and try out the buttons that take you to the previous or next page, as well as the Home button that takes you back to the table of contents on the "Learn About the Park" page. Try out the links in the table of contents, and test the cross-references (e.g., "see 'Sunset Cruises' on page 4") on the "About the Park" page. Do you think the various navigational controls do a good job of leading you through the document?

If you click the URL on the Directions page, you'll receive an alert (**Figure 2.3**). You won't see this alert if you're viewing a Web-hosted SWF in a browser. This is meant to protect you from malicious code being invoked by a link in a SWF file. If you wish to examine your current Flash Player Security settings, click the Settings button.

Figure 2.3 Attempt to exercise a Web link in a locally stored SWF, and you'll be intercepted by the Flash Player Security alert. Click the Settings button to launch the Settings Manager.

When you click the Settings button, you'll be taken to a Web page and prompted to change your local Flash viewing settings (**Figure 2.4**). As the link itself informs you, what looks like just a screen shot at the top of the page is in fact the Flash Player Settings Manager.

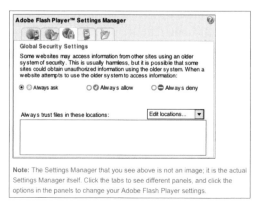

Figure 2.4 The Settings Manager allows you to control how Web links are handled while you're viewing a SWF file.

If you'd prefer to not alter your Flash Player settings (and, for safety's sake, it's a good idea not to), but would like to test the URL hyperlink, you can view the SWF on the Web rather than locally: http://www.practicalia.net/bfpark. Notice that the document contains the same material as the printed piece, but redesigned for onscreen viewing.

Generating a Table of Contents

While a table of contents might seem like a print-centric concept, it can serve a valuable purpose in a multipage interactive file. With just a bit of work up front, InDesign can generate a table of entries that are automatically hyperlinked to content in the document (hence the term *table of contents*). You're about to see how easy it is to build a table of contents—and the secret ingredient is the paragraph style.

1. Launch InDesign CS5. If you haven't already copied the **Ch_2_Exercise** folder to your hard drive, do that now. In the **Ch_2_Exercise** folder, open **BF_Start.indd**. Save the file as **BF_Working.indd** in the same folder before you start modifying it.

2. First, you'll create a table of contents that will provide dynamic links enabling the reader to jump to topics within the document. InDesign uses paragraph styles to identify text to be harvested for a TOC. Navigate to page 3, select the Type tool, and click in the text "About the Park." Choose Window > Styles > Paragraph Styles. In the Paragraph Styles panel, the Topics paragraph style is highlighted. That's the style you'll be looking for as you construct the TOC. Don't worry, InDesign will do all the heavy lifting for you.

3. Go to page 2; this is where you'll place the TOC text. Choose **Layout** > Table of Contents Styles.

4. In the Table of Contents Styles panel that appears, click the New button. Creating a new style allows you to name the style and leave the Default style untouched. The New Table of Contents Style dialog appears (**Figure 2.5**). Click the More Options button so you see the panel in the mode shown below.

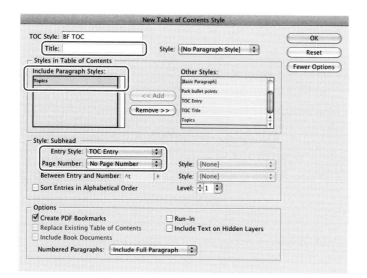

Figure 2.5 Setting up the Table of Contents style.

Use the following settings:

- In the Title field, delete the default text; InDesign won't generate title text.

- In the Include Paragraph Styles section, select the Topics style in the right column and click the Add button (or just double-click the Topics style name; you may have to scroll down in the list to find it). This tells InDesign, "Find all text tagged with the Topics style and add it to the TOC."

- Tell InDesign how to format the TOC content. For Entry Style, choose TOC Entry (a style already created in the document), and for Page Number, select No Page Number.

Click OK. At this point, you've created the recipe InDesign uses to generate the TOC, but you haven't set things in motion yet.

5. Now you'll generate the TOC text. Choose Layout > Table of Contents. In a case of page-layout déjà vu, it seems that you were just here a minute ago. It's InDesign's polite way of saying "I know you want to make a TOC, but here's one last chance to change your settings." Click OK, and InDesign gives you a loaded text cursor.

6. Click inside the ghosted text frame and view the table of contents. If you have a red overset text indicator, don't panic—it's just a leftover paragraph return. While it won't result in an incorrect link, it may mess up the vertical alignment of the TOC within the frame, so it's worth fixing. Choose Type > Show Hidden Characters so you can see the extra paragraph return, and then select and delete it.

7. To test the table of contents links, open the Preview panel (Window > Interactive > Preview), and click the Preview Document Mode button (⊡). This allows you to view the entire document, rather than just the current spread, and lets you test internal document links. Click the Play button (▶) in the Preview panel to build the preview. The first page appears, and the Luna moth flies across from right to left. Using the page controls at the bottom of the Preview panel, go to page 2, and then click the **Park Activities** link; it should take you to page 5 of the document in the Preview panel.

8. You knew to click the TOC link because you were instructed to do so; a reader might not suspect that they should do that. That's why there's a bit of instruction above the ghosted text frame: "Click to view topics." Include such little bits of guidance in your own documents so the unsuspecting reader knows what to do. All of your work in creating the TOC would be lost if the reader had no idea the entries were clickable.

Now you see why paragraph styles are for more than just controlling the appearance of text; they're also a mechanism for tagging text so you can use it as the basis for a TOC. And in an upcoming section, you'll use paragraph styles as part of creating cross-references. Save the file, and keep it open for the next section.

Creating Navigation Buttons

Readers can use the clickable TOC entries to get to a specific topic in the document, but what if they just want to page through the document on their own? How can they get back to the TOC? InDesign can include cute little "page curl" effects on the corners, but unless the user suspects that the page corners are hot spots, this isn't helpful. And the page corners don't offer any way to pages other than the previous or next page. You need to provide a more flexible system of navigation.

Buttons can act as triggers for a wide variety of functions, and can change their appearance based on their state (up, down, rollover). You'll spend more quality time with buttons in a later chapter, but this exercise will let you get acquainted with some of the possibilities buttons afford.

Figure 2.6 Because the buttons are master page objects, they can't be edited on the document page without unlocking.

1. If necessary, navigate to page 2. Open the Layers panel (Window > Layers), and make the **Buttons** layer visible by clicking in the "eyeball" column of the Layers panel. Three buttons appear on the page; currently, they all have the same appearance, but you'll change both their appearance and their function.

2. You can't select the buttons on page 2; the dotted border indicates that they are master page items (**Figure 2.6**). You could unlock the buttons and modify them, but then you'd have to do the same thing on all pages. It makes more sense to just edit the buttons once on the master page.

   In the Pages panel (Window > Pages), double-click the A-Master page icon. Now you can edit the buttons' appearance, and give them something to do.

3. All three buttons use the same Adobe Illustrator artwork, NavButtons.ai. While each button could have been created from a separate Illustrator file, stacking up all the artwork in one file means you just have to manage one file. You can use Object Layer Options in InDesign to control layer visibility within Illustrator, Photoshop, and placed PDF files. Select the left button, and then choose Object > Object Layer Options. In the Object Layer Options panel, turn off the visibility for the **next** and **home** layers, leaving only the **prev** layer visible (**Figure 2.7**), and then click OK.

Figure 2.7 Use Object Layer Options to control the visibility of layers in Illustrator, Photoshop, or PDF files.

4. Select the right button, and use Object Layer Options to turn off the **home** and **prev** layers, leaving only the **next** layer visible. The middle button's appearance is OK as it is, so you don't have to do anything to it yet.

5. Now the buttons look the part, but they aren't truly buttons yet. The "prev" button will take readers to the previous page, the "next" button will take them to the next page, and the "home" button will take them back to the TOC page. Select the "prev" button, and then open the Buttons

panel (Window > Interactive > Buttons). To convert the selected object to a button, you can either choose Object > Interactive > Convert to Button, or click the Convert to Button icon (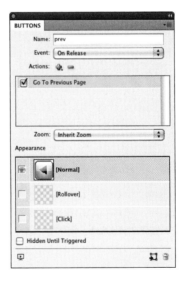) on the bottom of the Buttons panel. (You can also select the object in the page, and then right-click and choose Interactive > Convert to Button from the contextual menu that appears.) Now the Buttons panel comes to life, and you can give the button something to do.

6. Name the button **prev** rather than using the default name InDesign assigns. For Event, choose On Release; this is the instant you release the mouse button after clicking, and it's when a user expects something to happen. Click the plus sign next to Actions, and then select Go To Previous Page from the list of possible actions (**Figure 2.8**). Notice how many actions are available, and note that the list contains two sublists: actions that are SWF-only, and actions that are PDF-only. The top part of the list contains actions that work in either export format.

Figure 2.8 Assign the Go to Previous Page action to the On Release event of the "prev" button.

7. Select the "next" button object, and convert it to a button using either method described above. Name the button **next**, and for Action, choose the Go to Next Page action. If you like, check your work so far by running a preview in the Preview panel.

8. The "home" button will take users back to the TOC on page 2. Convert the object to a button, and name it **home**. In the Buttons panel, choose the Go to Page action from the SWF Only portion of the action list, and type **2** in the page field. Leave the other settings at their default values.

9. The cover page will need a "next page" button to lead the reader into the file, so copy the **next** button to the clipboard, and then double-click the page 1 icon in the Pages panel to go to page 1. Make sure the Buttons layer is still targeted in the Layers panel, and paste the button on the cover page. Reposition the button so it follows the text "Click here to get started..." (**Figure 2.9**).

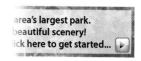

Figure 2.9 The "next page" button on the cover invites readers into the document.

10. Test all your buttons in the Preview panel, and fix anything that's gone awry. Note that you don't have to unlock the buttons on the document pages; they'll function just fine in all the pages as master objects. If all the buttons are behaving, save the file and leave it open for the next section. Or close the file and take a break.

Creating a Rollover Effect

When you want to display multiple large images in a small page, sometimes the best way is to not show them all at once, but provide small thumbnails as triggers to display the large images one by one, using a rollover effect.

A rollover is accomplished by using buttons, and consists of two pieces: a target button to contain the graphic you want to temporarily display, and a button to trigger the appearance of the target button. The mechanism is referred to as *Show/Hide Buttons* in InDesign. The effect can be activated by clicking the trigger button, or by rolling over the button area. In this document, you'll use the rollover effect.

1. Go to page 4 of the document, and open the Preview panel if it isn't already open. Change the preview mode to Preview Spread Mode ( ) so you don't have to wade through the full document preview to see what's happening on page 4. Note the instruction built right into the page: "Roll over a thumbnail for a larger view." Test the existing rollovers; as you roll over a thumbnail, a larger version of the image appears, accompanied by a text frame with information about the image or the park feature it represents. As you roll over the next thumbnail, the previous large image disappears, because the button action of the thumbnail is set to show one image while hiding all the other images.

2. Now that you've seen the desired effect, you'll set up a rollover action of your own. Zoom out until you can see the image and text frame in the pasteboard to the left of the page. Select both frames and group them (Object > Group). Then, move the grouped objects into the page and position them to match the other large images and text frames. You don't have

to be exact—remember, the other frames disappear, so no two frames appear simultaneously.

3. The large image and text frame need to become a button so their visibility can be controlled by another button—the other half of the two-member button team. Open the Buttons panel (Window > Interactive > Buttons), and reselect the grouped large image and text frame if necessary. Convert the group to a button by one of the methods you learned earlier, and name the button **dairy**. Check the Hidden Until Triggered option in the Buttons panel so the image won't appear until you want it to.

4. Now you'll create the button that triggers the appearance of the dairy farm image. Select the dairy farm thumbnail (the last image on the right in the row of thumbnails), and convert it to a button. Name the button **showdairy**, choose the On Roll Over event, and assign the Show/Hide Buttons action. Note that this thumbnail button needs to accomplish several things. It needs to show the large dairy graphic and it needs to force any other large graphics to hide, so it needs to address the behavior of multiple target buttons. The Show/Hide controls can be a bit confusing at first glance, so a decoder can be helpful (**Figure 2.10**).

Figure 2.10 Show/Hide Buttons controls. The "X" option means "leave it alone."

— Retain button's existing visibility
— Hide target button
— Make target button visible

- The solid eyeball icon means "make the target button visible."

- The crossed-out eyeball icon means "hide the target button."

- The "X" means "leave the target button alone; use its existing visibility setting."

5. Just setting the target button (**dairy**) to show isn't enough. You also have to hide the other large graphics that shouldn't be visible when the dairy graphic is visible, and you have to make sure that no other buttons are adversely affected. It's a bit tedious, especially since the Buttons panel doesn't allow you to expand the list of current buttons; you can see only three of them simultaneously in the claustrophobic little Visibility section

of the Buttons panel. (Let's hope this is fixed in a future release.) As you scroll through the list of buttons, use the settings shown in **Figure 2.11**. Essentially, you're making the large dairy graphic visible, hiding all the other large graphics in the spread, and making sure you don't accidentally hide the other thumbnail buttons or the navigation buttons.

6. After you've set the visibility options for all the necessary buttons, preview the results. Fix any problems, and preview one last time. Once you get the hang of "hide this, show that," the creation of rollovers is conceptually easy, if somewhat tedious.

7. Whew! This would be a good time for a break. I'm hungry—how about you? Save the file, and leave it open for the next section (or close it if you've had enough scrolling and clicking for one day).

Creating a Cross-Reference

While buttons can lead a reader from page to page, sometimes you want to provide more specific control. In a printed piece, cross-references can lead a reader to related information. They can serve the same purpose in an interactive document, with one added advantage—cross-references are actually clickable hyperlinks that take the reader immediately to the target content.

1. Navigate to page 3, and in the bullet point about Lake Baker, note the text in parentheses: "see 'Sunset Cruises' on page 4." While you could just type that text, it wouldn't translate to a clickable hyperlink in the exported SWF without some extra work on your part. A *cross-reference*, however, is easy to generate and automatically becomes a clickable hyperlink. (Subliminal message: Paragraph styles are your friends.)

2. Navigate to page 4 to find out how this cross-reference was generated. Because there are multiple frames stacked up on the page, it's hard to dig down and select the Sunset Cruise frame. But you can get an idea of what's going on. Choose the Type tool, and then click somewhere in the large italic **Lake Baker** text (not the small caption under the thumbnail). Check in the Paragraph Styles panel or the Control panel, and you'll see that the text uses the Subhead paragraph style. You'll recall from the section on creating a table of contents that paragraph styles are a tagging mechanism.

3. You'll create a cross-reference that goes hunting for text using the Subhead style. Go back to page 3, and zoom in on the bullet point about touring the authentic turn-of-the-century dairy farm. Switch to the Type tool if

Figure 2.11 Use this as a guide for setting up the Show/Hide options for the "showdairy" thumbnail button.

necessary, and click at the end of the paragraph. Type a space, and then choose Type > Hyperlinks & Cross-References > Insert Cross-Reference. The New Cross-Reference dialog opens (**Figure 2.12**).

Figure 2.12 In the New Cross-Reference dialog, you're creating a recipe for a cross-reference. Choose a target paragraph style, and then modify the cross-reference format if you wish.

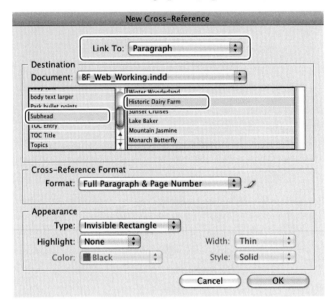

4. In the New Cross-Reference dialog, you specify whether InDesign should find text tagged with a particular paragraph style (the most common option) or text that's been earmarked as a text anchor (a manually created target). In the Destination section, specify the Subhead style in the left column, and all paragraphs using that style are then displayed in the right column. Scroll if necessary in the right column, and select Historic Dairy Farm from the list. This creates a dynamic hyperlink between the origin of the cross-reference on page 3 and its target on page 4. Leave the dialog open; you're going to change the cross-reference format in the next step.

5. Click the small pencil icon ( ) next to the Format pull-down so you can modify the definition for the format of the generated cross-reference text. The Cross-Reference Formats dialog appears (**Figure 2.13**). In the Definition field, click at the beginning of the line of code describing the cross-reference formula, and type an opening parenthesis. Click at the end of the line and type a closing parenthesis. The existing cross-references have manual parentheses, but including them in the cross-reference definition can save time in long documents; you'll fix the manual parentheses in a bit.

6. Check the Character Style option and choose the x-ref italic character style. Click OK; you can already see the change being applied to the cross-reference entries in the document. Click OK again to exit the New Cross-Reference dialog.

7. Delete the extraneous parentheses around the cross-references in the page, leaving only the parentheses that were created by the cross-reference definition. Put the Preview panel in Document Preview mode and test the cross-references; clicking one should take you to the target page.

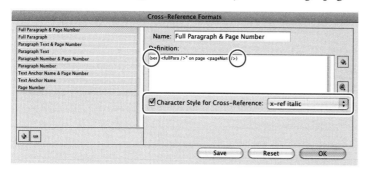

Figure 2.13 Examine the code in the Definition field, and it quickly makes sense. Here, you add opening and closing parentheses to the recipe and specify the character style to be used.

8. What happens if the target of a cross-reference changes? That's the beauty of creating cross-references the way you just did—they're dynamic. Test this by going to page 4 and changing the word "Historic" to "Authentic." Immediately, a yellow alert triangle appears next to the entry in the New Cross-References dialog (**Figure 2.14**). If the dialog is not showing, choose Window > Type & Tables > Cross-References. Click the Update icon (🔄) to update the cross-reference. Save the file and keep it open; there's just a bit more work to do.

NOTE: Occasionally a cross-reference becomes stubborn, and displays a red "Missing" flag, even though it's only been modified. Try undoing your change, saving the file, and tackling it again. It usually behaves the second time around (and no, I don't know why).

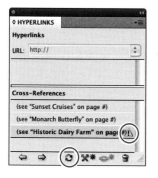

Figure 2.14 A yellow triangle indicates an out-of-date cross-reference. Click the Update icon to fix it.

Don't be intimidated by the Definition field in the Cross-Reference Formats dialog. If you're curious, it's not too hard to look at the definition and the text that's generated and figure out how the recipe

```
(see "<fullPara />" on page <pageNum />)
```

translates to:

(see "Authentic Dairy Farm" on page 4)

Explore the options available via the "plus" and "@" icons next to the Definition field, too.

Creating a Web Link

If you want to direct the reader to a Web site for more information, it's easy to provide a hyperlink in your document. If the text is already in the format of a URL, it's painless.

1. Go to page 6, select the Type tool, and then select the URL text, **http:// www.bfparkonline.net**. You don't even have to copy that text to the clipboard; just leave it highlighted.

2. If the Hyperlinks panel isn't open, choose Window > Interactive > Hyperlinks. From the Hyperlinks panel menu, choose New Hyperlink from URL. That's all there is to it—you can see the new hyperlink in the panel, and you're done. If you're curious about the option "Convert URLs to Hyperlinks," yes, it does indeed search for URL-formatted text in selected text, a story, or the entire document, and automatically creates hyperlinks for you. How cool is that?

3. Save the file, and keep it open for the last steps.

Exporting to SWF

All the hard work is done; now it's time to share the results. If you have a hosted Web site, you upload the finished files using your customary upload procedures, and view the SWF online. If not, you can view the local file.

1. Check your document thoroughly. Set the Preview panel to Preview Document Mode, and check all the internal links. Test the buttons and rollovers to make sure everything works as it should. Save the file.

2. Create a folder named **bfpark** in the **Ch_2_Exercise** folder or, if you prefer, in another location on your computer. Choose File > Export, navigate to the new **bfpark** folder, and select Flash Player (SWF) as the format. Name the SWF **bfpark.swf** and click Save.

3. The Export SWF dialog appears (**Figure 2.15**). Leave the settings at the defaults, but take this opportunity to familiarize yourself with some of the options. Click OK. Because the View SWF After Exporting option is checked by default, your default browser should launch when the export process is finished, and you can view the results.

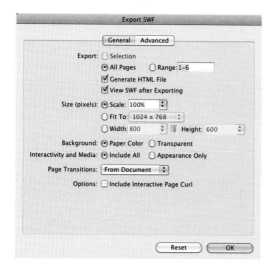

Figure 2.15 For this document, use the default SWF export settings. Make sure the Interactive Page Curl is not checked.

Of course, the animations and some of the rollover effects were already in place when you began working on this file, but think of the new skills you now have. You can create cross-references, generate a table of contents, assign actions to buttons, and create hyperlinks. You'll use those techniques constantly as you're bringing documents to life, whether you plan to export to SWF or interactive PDF.

Exporting to PDF

Interactive PDFs support some of the same functions available in SWF files. There's a good bit of overlap between the two formats, but they're not identical. Export your exercise file to interactive PDF and examine the results.

1. Choose File > Export, select Adobe PDF (Interactive) for the format, name the file bfpark.pdf, and save the PDF in the Ch_2_Exercise folder. Use the default settings, and wait for the finished PDF to be displayed. You'll receive an alert that the Go To Page button action isn't supported in PDF (**Figure 2.16**); this refers to the "Home" button that takes readers back to the TOC page. If you intend to export to PDF as well as SWF, you can provide equivalent functionality by creating a Text Anchor hyperlink on the TOC page and setting the Home button's action to a Go to Destination action with the text anchor as the destination.

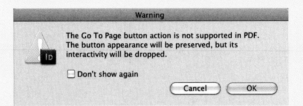

Figure 2.16 You're warned that the Go To Page button action doesn't translate to PDF. If you wish to export your file to interactive PDF, you can use a Go to Destination action instead.

2. Examine the PDF. While the flying moth and spinning daisy animations didn't survive the trip, the remaining interactive functions work. This gives you some idea of the overlap between SWF and PDF capability (and some of the shortfalls in PDF support).

If you want to post your SWF on your own Web site for testing, you may want to include the companion HTML file that is generated with the SWF; think of it as a rudimentary life support system for your SWF, making it easy to launch. (And, of course, remember that the graphics and text in the exercise file are just for tutorial use.)

Chapter 3

Multimedia

First, a little background on multimedia content in Adobe InDesign.

We've been able to place video and audio in InDesign since CS2, when we were thrilled to be able to export to interactive PDF. However, the PDF format had one limitation: Before Adobe Acrobat 9, the viewer had to have an appropriate multimedia interpreter on their system, external to Acrobat. So, for example, if a viewer attempted to play a QuickTime movie embedded in a PDF without the QuickTime viewer installed on their computer, they were out of luck. All they saw was an error message. Acrobat 9 and Adobe Reader 9 rectified this shortfall by including the ability to view video without needing an external player.

In InDesign CS4, we were given the option to export to SWF, but the SWF-iness of the export was mainly limited to cute page curls, clickable buttons, QuickTime movies, and page transitions. With CS5, you can now export a SWF with full support for the smaller, more modern Flash video formats, as well as MP3 audio files. If the viewer has the Adobe Flash plug-in for their browser, they'll be able to view your multimedia content in its full glory.

In this chapter's exercise, you'll add video and audio to a promotional piece for a fictional city's attractions. You'll dig a bit deeper into some of the concepts you explored in Chapter 1.

Video

If a picture is worth a thousand words, how much is a video worth? A short tutorial video can clearly convey a complex procedure, often better than written instructions. Or a video can be a great companion to text, bringing the topic to life or expanding on the written word.

Video Formats

TIP: If you'd like to look at the finished version of this project, you'll find the final InDesign file and the exported SWF (and supporting HTML file) in the **Finished File** folder inside the Ch_3_Exercise folder.

InDesign CS5 assumes you'll want to export to SWF or FLA, so it may display a cautionary message if you try to place some types of legacy video content, such as older versions of QuickTime (.mov). H.264-encoded content, such as MP4, is OK. AVI and MPEG aren't supported by Flash, and thus are not viable for projects you'll be exporting to FLA or SWF. If you intend to export to SWF or FLA, you should obtain versions of the desired video in an acceptable format, or convert your existing assets to FLV or F4V.

If you have Creative Suite Design Premium, Web Premium, or Production Premium, you have Adobe Media Encoder (a stand-alone application that is installed with Flash, Premiere Pro, After Effects, Soundbooth, and Encore), which will enable you to convert many other video formats to FLV or F4V. If you don't have Adobe Media Encoder, a quick Web search will unearth a number of media conversion programs, many of them attractively priced at $free.

In the first part of this exercise, we'll look at what happens when you import a video in Ye Olde QuickTime format.

1. Launch InDesign, navigate to the **Ch_3_Exercise** folder, and open **CityCenterStart.indd**. Save the file as **CityCenterWorking.indd** in the same folder. Choose the Interactive workspace (or your modified version of it, if you have moved panels around to suit you).

2. Page through the document. Navigation buttons are already in place, and the table of contents has been automatically generated so that the entries will be hyperlinked to their destination in the exported SWF. There are hints on several pages about the media files you'll place: an audio file on page 3, videos on pages 4 and 5.

3. View page 4 of the CityCenter file. In the Layers panel, make sure the **multimedia** layer is unlocked and selected. Choose File > Place, navigate to the **Multimedia Content** folder inside the exercise folder, and select **butterfly.mov**. Because this QuickTime file is ancient (in computer years, anyway), InDesign reacts to it like a two-year-old reacts to broccoli, and displays an alert (**Figure 3.1**). However, you can bully your way past the alert, click Continue, and place the file by clicking in the page. InDesign assumes you know what you're doing, and allows it because of the possibility that you're going to export the file to interactive PDF, which supports QuickTime content (provided the viewer is using Acrobat or Reader version 9, or has QuickTime installed on their system to serve as an external viewer).

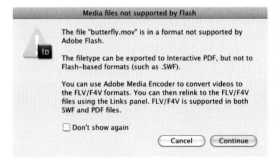

Figure 3.1 Attempt to place a video in any format other than FLV or F4V, and you're advised that it won't be supported by Flash. The QuickTime format is, however, supported in interactive PDF, so you will be allowed to place it despite the alert.

4. After all that, undo the movie import or delete the placed movie. The previous step was just to show you the alert you might encounter, so it won't alarm you in the future. Now you'll place the actual video, a short piece showing otters frolicking. Choose File > Place, navigate to the **Multimedia Content** folder, and select **OtterMovie.f4v**. Click in the page (don't click and drag) to place the video, and position it in the upper-right corner of the page, just inside the top and right edges of the page.

5. Open the Media panel (Window > Interactive > Media) to modify the settings for the placed movie (**Figure 3.2**). Since you'll use a button to trigger the movie, leave the Play on Page Load option unchecked. Because you don't want the movie to cover up the sea anemone photo in the background until it plays, set the Poster option to None. Choose SkinOverAll

from the Controller pull-down, and choose the Show Controller on Rollover option. The SkinOverAll option provides all options, including play, stop, pause, mute, and full-screen play (hence the "all" in the option name). You may want to experiment with the controllers to find which ones you find most useful.

6. The text "Play Otter Movie" is in a text frame that has already been converted to a button, but it has no attached action. In the Layers panel, unlock the **Buttons** layer, and select the **Play Otter Movie** button in the page. In the Buttons panel (Window > Interactive > Buttons), click the plus sign by Actions, and choose the Video option. Since the otter movie is the only video, it's automatically selected as the target, and the default Play action is selected as the action. Click the Preview icon (🖳) in the Buttons panel, or choose Window > Interactive >

Figure 3.2 Choosing the settings for the otter movie. Set the Poster option to None, so the still frame from the movie doesn't cover up the background photograph.

Preview to open the Preview panel. Test the button in the Preview panel. Does it launch the video? Roll over the video to see the options offered by the SkinOverAll controller you chose. Save the file and keep it open.

Controllers

When you place an FLV, F4V, or H.264-encoded file, you can choose from the long list of controllers in the Media panel. The Show on Rollover option displays the controls only when the user moves the mouse over the video (so they don't obscure the playback). If the video is a legacy file (such as MPEG or AVI), you'll only be able to add a basic controller with play, pause, start, and stop controls (no audio controls). Placed SWF files may have their own embedded controller skins. Use the Preview panel to check controller appearance and behavior. Custom controller skins can be created in Flash Professional, saved as SWF files, and stored in the Presets > Multimedia > **FLVPlayback Skins** folder inside the InDesign application folder.

Posters

By default, InDesign represents a placed video by displaying the first frame of the video. You can also use the "standard" poster, which is a graphic resembling a filmstrip. For the otter movie, you set the poster to None so the background photo wasn't covered up. There are also other options. You can scrub through the video in the Media panel, select any frame in the video, and designate it as the representative poster. As you saw in Chapter 1, you can also specify a separate image for the poster. This is a great option if you plan to use the document for both print and Web; you can place a high-resolution poster image appropriate for print, and the image will be optimized for Web viewing when the project is exported to SWF—it's the best of both worlds. You'll experiment now with the poster options for another video.

1. Go to page 5 of the CityCenter document. Choose File > Place, navigate to the **Multimedia Content** folder, select **PeacockMovie.f4v**, and click to the left of the large text frame describing the wildlife preserve to place it. (It may take the video a few seconds to "settle in" and allow you to select it.) Position the video at the lower left of the page, lining up its bottom edge with the bottom of the text frame.

2. In the Control panel, choose [Paper] for the stroke attribute of the frame containing the video. This will add a 1-pixel white stroke around the video, to set it apart from the green background photograph. If you like, increase the weight of the white stroke to suit you.

3. In the Media panel, scrub the playhead to about the 5.5 second mark to show the peacock's tail facing the viewer (**Figure 3.3**). Click the Use Current Frame icon (icon) to designate the chosen frame as the poster. Check the results in the Preview panel.

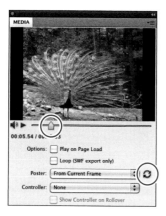

Figure 3.3 Scrub through the video to find a better frame to serve as a poster, and pin it down with the Use Current Frame icon to the right of the Poster pull-down.

4. That's certainly an improvement, but if this document will be used for both print and Web purposes, a high-resolution image might be even better. Before you bring in the image, however, take a look at the Links panel (Window > Links); **PeacockMovie.f4v** is listed as a link, just like a placed graphic. This is what you'd expect, but it's interesting to notice what happens when you assign an image as a replacement poster. If necessary, reselect the peacock video frame and, in the Media panel, select the Choose Image option from the Poster pull-down. Navigate to the **Multimedia Content** folder and select **PeacockPoster.psd**. It's about the right size to fit neatly in the frame. Now, look at the Links panel. There are two entries for the selected frame: one for the video, and one for the imported image poster (**Figure 3.4**). Think of them as roommates in the frame.

Figure 3.4 Frames containing both a video and an image poster are represented by two entries in the Links panel.

5. Choose SkinOverAll from the Controller pull-down, and check the option for Show Controller on Rollover (this displays the controller only when the viewer mouses over the video while it's playing; the controller will not show if the user mouses over the area of the video when it isn't active).

Navigation Points

Sometimes you want to draw the viewer's attention to a particular part of a video, especially if it's a long video containing multiple topics or scenes. You can add *navigation points* to a video, which can be invoked by buttons or upon page load to ensure that the viewer sees what you think is important. You'll create three navigation points: one for the full display of the peacock's tail, one for his distinctive call, and one that shows the beginning of his festive mating dance.

1. Select the peacock movie frame. Even though the poster image seems to cover the movie, selecting the frame still lets you address the movie and control its attributes. In the Media panel, scrub the playhead under the video preview until you reach approximately the 5.5 second mark. It may be difficult to move the playhead smoothly; you can use keyboard arrows to advance/reverse the time in the playback line, but the preview may not update. Yes, it's a little kludgy. Sometimes it's easier to just play the video in the Media panel and note the timecode for the moment you want to freeze. The time is displayed below the playback line, showing the current time position in the video, followed by the total time length of the video. Just try to get close to the 5.5 second mark on the playback line. When you reach the approximate moment of the peacock's tail unfurling for the first time, the readout below the playline will be something like 00:5.55/00:33.53, indicating that you're at the 5.5 second mark of a 33.5 second video.

Figure 3.5 To create a navigation point, scrub to the correct part of the video and click the "+" icon below the Navigation Points area.

2. Once you've reached the approximate 5.5 second mark on the playline, click the plus sign below the Navigation Points area to create a new navigation point. It's initially named Point 1, but the name is highlighted so you can immediately rename it. Name this first navigation point **tail feathers** (**Figure 3.5**).

3. Scrub to about the 10 second mark on the playline, and create a navigation point for the peacock's distinctive call. Name this point **mating call**. If you accidentally create a navigation point that you don't want, select the point in the list and click the minus sign to delete it.

4. Create a navigation point at approximately the 23 second mark, to showcase the peacock's mating dance. He spins to show the back of his splendid tail, and does some fancy wing work. Name this navigation point **dance**.

5. Now, it's time to trigger the movie at the three navigation points you created. You'll accomplish this by creating buttons that become hot spots over the text on the page. In the Layers panel, target the **Buttons** layer. Using the Rectangle Frame tool (⊠), draw a rectangle around the text "Click here to see the peacock's beautiful tail." Make the rectangle large enough to cover all the text, but keep the bottom of the rectangle very close to the baseline of the text. There will be a total of four buttons (one over each of the last four lines of text). You want them to be large enough to be easily clicked, but not so large that the user clicks the wrong one by mistake. Keep the rectangle selected.

NOTE: You can start playing a video at a designated navigation point, but you cannot use a navigation point as a stopping point. If users want to stop a movie, they'll have to use the Stop or Pause options in the video controller—another good reason to include a controller.

TIP: If you duplicate a button that contains an action that triggers a sound, video, or animation, the action is automatically removed from the duplicate. InDesign seems to feel that it's redundant to have more than one trigger for a multimedia event. Of course, you can manually add the action to the duplicate.

6. In the Buttons panel, click the Convert Object to a Button icon (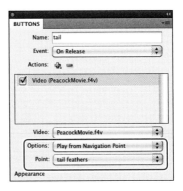). Name the button **tail**, click the plus sign by Actions, and select the Video action from the pull-down list. The peacock video is automatically selected, since it's the only video in the current spread (you can only trigger videos within a current spread). In the Options pull-down, choose Play from Navigation Point, and select **tail feathers** from the Point pull-down (**Figure 3.6**). Test the button in the Preview panel to make sure it triggers the video correctly from the chosen navigation point.

Figure 3.6 Choose the Play from Navigation Point option in the Buttons panel, and then you can select which navigation point to target.

7. Now you'll create a button named **play dance** for the dance navigation point. Drag a rectangle around the text "Click here to see the peacock's dance display," and convert the rectangle to a button. Set it to trigger the video at the **dance** navigation point.

TIP: InDesign supports streaming video in exported SWF and interactive PDF files. Select an empty frame (or a frame containing a local video that you want to replace), and choose Video From URL from the Media panel menu. The video format must be supported by the Flash Player.

8. You'll create a button named **mating call** for the mating call navigation point. Drag a rectangle around the text "Click here to hear the peacock's mating call," and convert the rectangle to a button. Set it to trigger the video at the **mating call** navigation point.

9. Create a button named **play** for the last line of text, "Click here to play the peacock movie." This will play the video from the beginning. Test all four buttons in the Preview panel, and then save the file and keep it open for the next section.

Adding Objects On Top of Video Content

You can place objects on top of video content to create interesting effects, such as corner decorations. You can even use this method to colorize part of a video, by applying a blending mode to an overlaying object (thanks to Jean-Claude Tremblay for pointing out that trick!). However, at least some of the video must be uncovered and clickable—it can't be completely covered by an object.

NOTE: If you have created interactive PDFs, you may be surprised to learn that you can place objects on top of video content in InDesign files destined for export to SWF. Acrobat handles video as floating content that appears in front of all other objects (except buttons).

1. In the Layers panel, select the **multimedia** layer. Choose File > Place, navigate to the **Multimedia Content** folder, and select **PeacockFeather.psd**. Click anywhere in the page to place the image. You're about to rotate and reposition it.

2. Now you'll rotate the feather clockwise. Just hover your cursor a bit outside one of the corners of the frame, and a two-headed curved arrow icon appears, indicating that you can now rotate the frame interactively. This is much more fun than having to switch to the Rotate tool. Rotate the feather and position it over the upper-left corner of the peacock video frame (**Figure 3.7**).

Figure 3.7 Position the feather over the corner of the video frame (we rotated to -58 degrees). It should add a bit of visual interest, without covering up important elements in the video.

3. Because the feather, the video poster, and the forest background are so similar in color, the artwork sort of all runs together. You'll add a glow around the peacock feather to make it easier to see. If necessary, reselect the feather, then right-click (Mac: Control-click) and choose Effects > Outer Glow from the contextual menu. In the dialog that follows, set the Opacity to 70%, and the size to 7 pixels (as always, feel free to stray from these settings to experiment). The feather should be more visible now, without being too obvious.

4. Test the file in the Preview panel. If the feather is covering up too much of the video, reposition the feather, reduce its size, or rotate it to a different angle—or do all three. It's your project, and ultimately it's up to you to decide when it looks satisfactory. Save the file and keep it open.

Audio

If you place a video containing an audio track into an InDesign file, the sound is not a separate entity; if the video plays, its audio track plays. But sometimes you'll want audio accents, such as music or chirping birds, in your projects.

Audio Formats and Settings

NOTE: Sounds can be placed out in the pasteboard and still function in an exported SWF file. However, a sound in the pasteboard is not included in an exported interactive PDF, and pasteboard contents are not included when a document is packaged.

Picking the audio format is easy: if you're exporting to SWF or FLA, you can only import audio files in MP3 format. Other formats are supported only if you export to interactive PDF. If you have Apple iTunes, Adobe Media Encoder, or Adobe Soundbooth, you can easily convert other audio formats to MP3. Or you can take advantage of the many free (or inexpensive) conversion applications available on the Web.

1. Go to page 3 of the document, which displays information about CityCenter Park. Choose File > Place, navigate to the **Multimedia Content** folder, select **WaterChimes.mp3**, and click OK. Place the file anywhere in the page. While you can choose from No Poster, Standard Poster, or an image in the Media panel, none of these will make the area of the placed audio visible or clickable in an exported SWF. This seems to be a bug (it works as expected in an exported interactive PDF). That's OK; we'll cheat.

2. In the Media panel, check the options for Play on Page Load and Stop on Page Turn. When the viewer clicks a navigation button at the bottom of the page, the audio track will stop abruptly. This is a brief audio clip, but if a long audio clip follows the viewer onto another page, it could still be playing when another audio or video clip is triggered.

3. Go to page 6 of the document. In the Layers panel, unlock the **Basics** layer. Select the red music clef in the page. In the Layers panel, click the small red square on the right side of the **Basics** layer, hold down the mouse button, and drag the red square up to the **Buttons** layer. This transplants the clef artwork frame to the Buttons layer. Lock the **Basics** layer and target the **Buttons** layer.

4. Choose File > Place, navigate to the **Multimedia Content** folder, select **Orchestra.mp3**, and click OK. Target the **multimedia** layer, click in the page—it doesn't matter where—and place the sound. When you're done, target the **Buttons** layer.

5. Rather than have the sound triggered when the viewer reaches this page, you'll set up a button so the viewer can choose when to listen to the City Center Orchestra. In the **Buttons** layer, select the red music clef frame, right-click (Mac: Control-click), and choose Interactive > Convert to Button from the contextual menu. A rectangular hot spot is created, surrounding the rotated clef frame, and the Buttons panel automatically opens. In the Buttons panel, name the button **Orchestra**, and click the plus sign next to the Actions label to choose the Sound option. Since the orchestra audio is the only one in the page, it's automatically selected, as is the Play option. Make sure that the Play on Page Load option is not selected, and please don't check the Loop option—that's just plain mean.

TIP: Videos and sounds appear in the **Timing** panel, so they can be controlled by delay and playing order options, just like animations. You'll learn more about the Timing panel in Chapter Four, "Animation."

6. You've been checking your work throughout the project, but it's always advisable to export the project and test it in multiple browsers. Save the file as **CityCenterDone.indd** in the **Ch_3_Exercise** folder. Choose File > Export and select the Flash Player (SWF) format. Accept the default settings, but make sure the Interactive Page Curl option is not checked.

7. As you view the project in your default browser, test all the navigation buttons at the bottom of the page; you'll learn how to create such buttons in Chapter 5. Make sure the audio and video content play as you expect. If you need to tweak anything, modify the InDesign file, save it, and re-export it, overwriting the earlier files. When you're finished, you can save and close the file.

As you've seen, it's as easy to place music or movies in an InDesign document as it is to place images and text. You can trigger a video with a button or a simple page turn and greatly enhance the user's viewing experience. And now you know it's much easier than it looks!

Chapter 4

Animation

While previous versions of InDesign allowed you to create hyperlinks and import video and sound files, the InDesign document itself was static; none of the page content wiggled or barked. While InDesign CS4 introduced the ability to import SWF files and to export to the SWF format, the resulting SWF was still just a container for content that had to be created elsewhere. But InDesign CS5 allows you to do so much more—now, page content itself can be animated. Here's where the real fun begins!

What Can Be Animated?

Any text frame, graphics frame, or empty frame (or group of frames) can be animated. As you saw in Chapter 3, "Multimedia," a frame containing an FLV or FV4 video can be animated, but the video inside the frame won't play until the animated frame calms down and stops doing whatever it's doing. However, remember that a frame containing a placed SWF file can be animated, and the animation inside the frame *will* play while its container is doing something else (as long as something triggers the SWF to play). Think of the fiendish possibilities!

Exploring the Possibilities

There's a great little guide to InDesign's animation capabilities built right into the application, but you have to do a little digging to find it. First, you have to find a script that ships with InDesign. The script generates an InDesign document containing examples of objects using many of the animation controls. You can examine each object's settings in the Animation and Timing panels and learn a lot.

1. To start your quest for the Animation Encyclopedia (its official name), open the Scripts panel (Window > Utilities > Scripts). You'll see two folders: **Application** and **User**. The **User** folder stores scripts you download to add to InDesign's functionality (the scripts displayed are those installed by the currently active computer user); the **Application** folder contains the scripts that ship with InDesign (**Figure 4.1**).

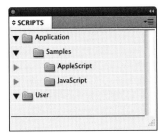

Figure 4.1 Sample scripts are supplied in two formats for Windows (JavaScript and VBScript) and two formats for Mac (JavaScript and AppleScript). All application scripts are available in both formats; only JavaScript is cross-platform.

2. You'll have to keep digging. Click the triangle next to the **Application** folder to view the **Samples** folder. Here's where the road forks: If you're using Windows, you'll see subfolders for **VBScript** and **JavaScript;** on the Mac, you'll have subfolders for **AppleScript** and **JavaScript.** The script selection is actually the same in both subfolders, so it doesn't matter which you select for the next step; you're almost there. Click the triangle

next to JavaScript, VBScript, or AppleScript, and there it is (finally): **AnimationEncyclopedia** (**Figure** 4.2).

Figure 4.2 You'll find the AnimationEncyclopedia script in the **JavaScript**, **AppleScript**, or **VBScript** folder (depending on your platform). You'll see VBScript on Windows, and AppleScript on the Mac. JavaScript is cross-platform.

3. Double-click the script to run it. InDesign takes the reins and builds a six-page document. It may not look very exciting at first (**Figure** 4.3), but it packs a secret punch. Preview the document and play along. Some objects require that you click them or the page, and some will be triggered when the page loads.

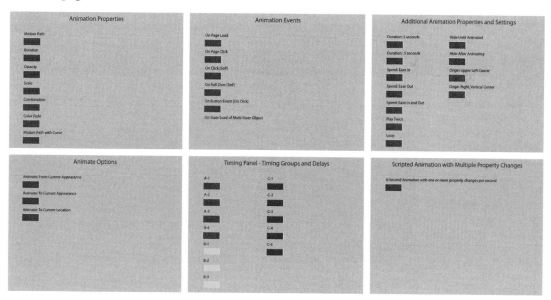

Figure 4.3 The design of the Animation Encyclopedia may not be compelling, but the beauty is under the hood. Preview this simple document, and prepare to be amazed.

The document that's created is named **Untitled.indd**; I suggest you save it as **AnimationEncyclopedia.indd** and put it in a safe place. You can learn a lot about InDesign's animation capabilities by examining the settings used by those little rectangles. Just so you know, page 6 of the document displays very complex behavior that's beyond what you can do with just the animation and timing settings; it's accomplished with scripting (as are the Color Fade and Combination effects on page 1). To give you an idea of its complexity, look at an excerpt from the JavaScript version of the Animation Encyclopedia script (**Figure 4.4**).

Figure 4.4 Scripting can accomplish complex animations far beyond what's possible with the motion and timing controls.

```
//Add rectangle.
var myRectangle1P6 = myMakeRectangle(myDocument.pages.item(5), [1.625,1,2
NoneSwatch, 0);
    //Set duration before adding keyframes when scripting animations
    myRectangle1P6.animationSettings.duration = 6;
    //Assumes 24 Frames Per Second (FPS)
    //23 = 1 second, 47 = 2 seconds, 71 = 3 seconds, 95 = 4 seconds, 119 = 5 seconds, 1
    mySetUnits(MeasurementUnits.points);
    //Note that the animation here is created with motionPath, which allows for se
    myRectangle1P6.animationSettings.motionPath = [[0, [[0, 0], [0, 0], [0, 0]]]
[200, 200]]], [119, [[0, 200], [0, 200], [0, 200]]], [143, [[0, 0], [0, 0], [0, 0]]]];
    mySetUnits(MeasurementUnits.inches);
    //Note that this animation allows setting multiple changes in opacity, scale and ro
    //correspond to points in the motion path. This functionality is not available i
    myRectangle1P6.animationSettings.rotationArray = [[0, 0], [23, 180], [47, 0]
    myRectangle1P6.animationSettings.scaleXArray = [ [0, 100.0 ], [23, 200.0], [47,
    myRectangle1P6.animationSettings.scaleYArray = [ [0, 100.0 ], [23, 0.0], [47, 100.
    myRectangle1P6.animationSettings.opacityArray = [ [0, 100.0 ], [23, 0.0], [47, 100.
    myRectangle1P6.animationSettings.plays = 1;
    myRectangle1P6.animationSettings.playsLoop = false;
    myRectangle1P6.animationSettings.easeType = AnimationEaseOptions.noEase;
    myRectangle1P6.animationSettings.transformOffsets = [0.5, 0.5];
    myRectangle1P6.animationSettings.designOption = DesignOptions.fromCurrentAp
    myRectangle1P6.animationSettings.initiallyHidden = false;
    myRectangle1P6.animationSettings.hiddenAfter = false;
```

Don't freak out—you're not expected to write code like this! All the behaviors you see on pages 1 through 5 of the encyclopedia—and many more—can be achieved by using the controls and options in the Animation and Timing panels. The inclusion of the over-the-top performance on page 6 is to expose you to the fact that animation, like every other operation in InDesign, is completely scriptable. For this and other reasons, it's a good idea to befriend a scripter and take him/her to lunch occasionally.

Events

An animation requires two components: the object or objects being animated, and an event to trigger the playing of the animation. The triggering event could be the click of a button, a click of the animated object itself, or just the loading of the page on which the animation was created. Now you'll do some exploring, so you can see how easy it is to make simple objects do your bidding.

On Page Load

The default animation-triggering event is the simplest: The animation plays when the reader reaches the page (or opens the document, if the page is the first—or only—page).

1. Launch InDesign, navigate to the **Ch_4_Exercises** folder, and open **Events_Start.indd**. Before changing anything in the file, resave the file as **Events_Working.indd**. If necessary, choose the Interactive workspace from the Control panel (unless you have a custom panel arrangement for the interactive panels and don't want to alter that).

2. Notice the caption beneath each object, describing the trigger that will set the object's animation in motion (**Figure 4.5**). Select one of the objects and look in the Animation panel; nobody home. You'll create the animations and set up the event triggers. If you're curious, you can preview a finished version of the file in the exercises folder (**Events_Done.indd**).

ON PAGE LOAD   ON PAGE CLICK   ON CLICK (SELF)   ON ROLL OVER (SELF)   ON BUTTON EVENT

Figure 4.5 The caption under each object specifies the event that will trigger the object's animation. You'll create each animation behavior and set up the event triggers.

3. Select the green globe with the "On Page Load" caption and open the Animation panel. Rename the object **GreenGlobe**. (It's helpful to give objects names you'll recognize when you set up animations.) While each object in this page is unique, how would you address the correct circle in a page full of circles? By its name, of course. By the way, renaming the object in the Animation panel also changes its name in the Layers panel (and vice versa).

4. In the Animation panel, choose Fly in from Top from the Preset pull-down menu. A charming lavender butterfly demonstrates the animation for you. The Event option should already be set to the default, On Page Load (**Figure 4.6**). If you don't see all the options, click the triangle to the left of Properties to reveal more of the panel. Leave all the other options at their defaults. Check the results in the Preview panel (Window > Interactive > Preview). Save the file and keep it open. There's more fun to be had.

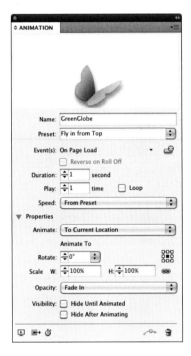

Figure 4.6 Set the GreenGlobe object to fly in from the top of the page on page load.

On Page Click

You may find that you rarely use the On Page Click event as a trigger for animation, since a reader probably wouldn't feel the urge to click the page unless invited to do so. Artwork or text would have to give the reader a hint, or nothing would ever happen. But you never know when it might come in handy, so here goes.

1. Select the embossed orange square, and then choose Fly Out > Fly Out Top from the Preset pull-down menu (the Fly Out Top option is available in the submenu of the Fly Out option).

2. The Events pull-down menu control isn't obvious; it's a tiny triangle about an inch to the right of the Event(s) label in the Animation panel, and it comprises about six pixels. Squint a bit, and you'll find it (**Figure 4.7**). The triangle is a small target, but you can activate it by clicking the name of the existing event: On Page Load. (You can also click a bit to the left of the pull-down triangle and activate it.)

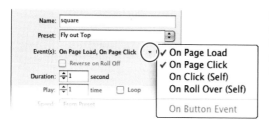

Figure 4.7 The Event options are available when you click the tiny triangle to the right of the Event(s) option. Could it be any more subtle?

Once you've found the miniature triangle, click it and choose On Page Click from the menu.

3. IMPORTANT: Choosing the On Page Click option does not override the original On Page Load trigger; this is easy to overlook when you're in a hurry. Go back to the same menu and select On Page Load to toggle it off. Otherwise, the orange square will fly upward when the page loads, before the user has an opportunity to click the page, thus spoiling the surprise. In the Preview panel, wait for the green globe to fly in from the top, and then click in the Preview panel to set the orange square in motion. Be sure to click in an empty part of the page (despite the temptation to click on the orange square) to prove to yourself that it's the page click that does the trick. Save the file and keep it open.

On Click (Self)

If you want the reader to click on an object to wake it up, use the On Click (Self) event. The term may seem odd; after all, the object can't click itself. But it just means that the animation is triggered by clicking the object itself, rather than by clicking an external trigger.

1. Select the red heart-shaped object, and change its name to **Heart** in the Animation panel. Choose the Pulse animation from the Preset pull-down (it's in the bottom part of the long list of presets).

2. Now that you've found the elusive Events pull-down triangle, choose the On Click (Self) option. Be sure to go back and toggle the default On Page Load option off.

3. Test the file in the Preview panel; click the heart and watch it beat hypnotically. If you like, experiment with the duration of the pulse, and set the number of times to 2 or 3. Remember this around Valentine's Day (or Halloween). Save the file and keep it open.

As with the On Page Click option, something has to lure the reader to click on the object to trigger its animation. While a "Click Me!" label might be a bit inelegant, something must provide a hint, or the heart will never have a chance to beat.

On Roll Over (Self)

Now that you know that "(Self)" refers to the animated object itself, it's obvious that the On Roll Over (Self) event triggers an animation when the reader rolls over the animated object. You'll use the rollover event to make the blue half-circle spin around.

1. Select the blue object, and change its name to **HalfCircle** in the Animation panel. Choose the On Roll Over (Self) event, and then choose the Rotate > Rotate 180° CW option from the Preset pull-down menu. Remember to toggle the On Page Load event off. Test the half-circle in the Preview panel.

2. Try holding the mouse on the half-circle, and you'll see that the half-circle keeps rotating. That's one oddity about using the rollover event as the trigger for an animation that keeps an object in the same location: If the user doesn't move the mouse away from the object, the animation is repeatedly triggered. Save the file and keep it open.

Note that when you choose the On Roll Over (Self) event, a new option appears in the Animation panel: Reverse on Roll Off. This would reverse (or undo) the animation move caused by the Roll Over event. For example, if the Reverse on Roll Off option is checked and you rotate an object 90 degrees clockwise by rolling over it, the object will rotate back to its original orientation when you roll off it.

On Button Event

One of the most common methods you'll use to trigger an animation is a button click. You must create the animation (even if it's just a temporary version of the animation) before setting up the button, or the button has nothing to hook up to. (In Chapter 5, "Button Up," you'll learn how to create cool button artwork in Adobe Photoshop, Adobe Illustrator, and Adobe InDesign.)

1. Select the purple doughnut shape. Name it **Doughnut** in the Animation panel, and select the Grow option from the Preset pull-down. Set the scale factor to 150%, and choose the On Page Load event to toggle it off, in preparation for triggering the growing animation with a button.

2. Select the gray button in the bottom right corner of the page, and open the Buttons panel (Window > Interactive > Buttons) to set it up. Choose the default On Release event, and click the plus sign next to Actions to select Animation (in the SWF section of the menu).

3. Note that when you select the Animation action, the panel changes in response, adding a pull-down menu that allows you to select which animation is triggered, and to select from options including Play, Stop, Pause, and Resume. Select the **Doughnut** animation and the default Play option. Test the file in the Preview panel. Export the file if you'd like to view it in a browser. You're finished with this exercise, so you can save the file for future reference and then close it.

TIP: You can also create a relationship between the animation and the button right in the Animation panel. Click the Create Button Trigger icon (⊡) in the Animation panel, and then click the button that will act as the trigger. If the trigger object is not yet a button, you're given the opportunity to make it a button.

Think about how the animated piece is presented, either in the Preview panel or in a browser. You knew where and what to click, because you were adding the interactive features. But would a reader, stumbling onto your Web page, know where to click? Probably not. This exercise was meant to familiarize you with the controls and options, not to create a final piece that would be published online. But when you start creating your own animations, you'll have to provide hints to the reader so they don't miss out on some of the fun, especially if the animated objects are hidden when the reader first views the document.

Combining Animations

If you were intrigued by the multiple behaviors of the object on page 6 of the Animation Encyclopedia, but don't have the time or inclination to learn scripting, you can cheat. I mean, use a workaround.

An animated object can be grouped with other objects, and then the group can be animated, resulting in a second behavior added to the original animation. Buttons can be grouped with other objects in a group that becomes animated, giving you the ability to make buttons move. You can keep nesting animations inside animations until… well, as long as your conscience will allow.

1. In the **Ch_4_Exercises** folder, open **MultiMoveStart.indd**. Resave the file as **MultiMoveWorking.indd** in the same folder. The objects in the page have already been named in the Layers panel, which will save you some

time (approximately half a second) when you animate them. If you like, preview the finished version of the project, **MultiMoveDone.indd**.

2. Select the yellow star with a solid red stroke. In the Animation panel, choose the Grow preset, set the Duration to 2 seconds, and set the final scale factor to 200%. Be sure that the center point is selected in the scale orientation control (▦) in the Animation panel, so the star scales up from the center. Test the growing star in the Preview panel.

3. Select the light-blue square, and send it behind the star in stacking order: Object > Arrange > Send to Back. Select the light-blue square and center it under the yellow star (Smart Guides can make this easy). If you're not sure the blue square and yellow star are perfectly centered, select them both, open the Align panel (Window > Object & Layout > Align), and use the vertical and horizontal center operations (**Figure 4.8**). It's even easier to use the alignment icons in the Control panel.

Figure 4.8 Make sure the yellow star is perfectly centered on the blue square by clicking the Align Horizontal Centers icon and then the Align Vertical Centers icon in the Align panel.

4. Now you'll start piling on the animations. Group the blue square and yellow star together, and snap the group to the lower-left corner of the page. In the Animation panel, rename the group **StarSquare**, choose the Fly In From Top preset, and set the Duration to 2 seconds. The intention is to have the star-and-square group drop in from the top of the page, while the star scales simultaneously. But when you preview the animation, it clearly needs more work. You need to modify the length of the fly-in from the top of the page, as well as synchronize the fly-in and the scaling of the star.

5. If necessary, reselect the group so you can see the bright green fly-in path (**Figure 4.9**). Notice that it has little nodes. Yes, this means that you can edit any motion path. Click the path (the "bulb" at the top is probably the easiest target), and you'll see a narrow bounding box appear around the path. The goal is to stretch the top anchor point on the path up to the top edge of the page. Pull up on the top anchor point—and it snaps back to its original position. Aargh! (This is a peculiarity of the Fly in from Top and Fly in from Bottom presets.)

Here's the trick: Switch to the Direct Selection tool (white arrow). The bounding box disappears, and the motion path now appears as a hairline. Click on the tiny top anchor point, hold down the Shift key (lest the path wander left or right), and drag straight up until you touch the top edge of the page. You can also set up the length and position of the motion path in the measurements fields in the Control panel, but you may find selecting and dragging easier and more intuitive.

6. The star should grow as the star-and-square group falls from the top of the page, so you'll have to synchronize the star's growth with the square's fall. Switch back to the black arrow, and reselect the group. In the Timing panel, Shift-click to select both the **tacky star** and **StarSquare** animations, and click the link icon to synchronize them (**Figure 4.10**). Now, the scaling of the star and the group's aerial drop will occur simultaneously. Preview the results, save the file, and keep it open for the grand finale.

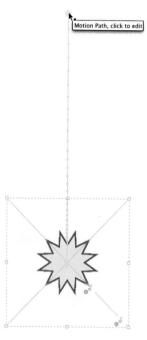

Figure 4.9 The anchor points provide a hint that you can edit the motion path just like any other Bézier path.

Figure 4.10 Select the **tacky star** and **StarSquare** animations and synchronize them by clicking on the small link icon at the bottom of the Timing panel.

TIP: There's a shortcut to the Timing panel at the bottom of the Animation panel: Just click the Timing panel icon (⚙).

7. Now you'll add another animation, to send the star-and-square group flying off the page to the right. Select the empty rectangle on the page, and move it to the lower-left corner so it's aligned with the star-and-square group; the lower-left corner of the group should be aligned with the lower-left corner of the page. Select all the objects and group them (Object > Group).

TIP: Sometimes it's easier to modify the behavior of an animation if you choose the Animation Proxy view mode. Click the Animation Proxy icon on the bottom of the Animation panel (▣→) to see "ghosts" of the object at the start and end points of the animation path.

8. In the Animation panel, name the new group **FinalGroup**, and choose the Fly Out > Fly Out Right preset. You'll have to edit the preset motion path so that the **FinalGroup** flies all the way off the right side of the page.

9. If necessary, select the **FinalGroup** object so you can see its bright-green motion path. Unlike the Fly in from Top motion path, this path can be edited without switching to the Direct Selection tool (only the Fly In from Top and Fly In from Bottom presets have this limitation). Select the path itself, click the green arrowhead on the end of the path, and drag the arrowhead to the right until it's far enough off the page that the star-and-square group will disappear at the end of its travel. Look up in the Control panel; the total length of the path (the "L" field) should be about 425 px.

10. You'll make one last change; rather than having the star-and-square group fade out as it exits, you'll keep it solid. In the Animation panel, change the Opacity setting from Fade Out to None. Preview the final animation, tweak if you want, and then save and close the file.

This is just a simple example, but it gives you an idea of what's possible without learning how to script InDesign. I don't mean to imply that this is a *good* thing to do, from a design standpoint; this is one of those "just because you can, doesn't mean you should" situations. The potential for garish, annoying animations is limitless. I feel guilty even showing this to you (you're welcome).

Motion Presets

As you probably noticed while working through the previous exercises, InDesign includes an extensive assortment of motion presets to get your content moving (**Figure 4.11**). The presets are the same ones you'll find in Adobe Flash CS5 Professional, and you can also import any custom presets that have been created in Flash Professional. You can create custom motion presets in InDesign, save them for future use, and share them with other InDesign users or Flash designers. There's just no end to the flying, dancing, bouncing fun you can have with motion settings.

Figure 4.11 How many motion presets ship with InDesign? Feast your eyes. And restrain yourself—you don't have to use every single one in your project. The motion presets below the dividing line include special effects such as multiple stops or disappearing in smoke.

But maybe that's not enough for you. Maybe you want more.

Motion Paths

If you want to make an object move along a more interesting path than just straight up or left to right, it's surprisingly easy to do: You just have to draw the path you want the object to follow. You can use the Line tool, the Pen tool, or the Pencil tool—anything that creates a Bézier path. The path can be a simple straight line or a complicated curlicue. The stroke attributes of the line aren't important; its appearance is discarded once it's designated as a motion path.

Creating a Custom Motion Preset

In this exercise, you'll work on a child's birthday party invitation, modifying existing presets and saving them as custom presets. You will also be creating several custom motion paths and saving their settings as custom presets.

1. Navigate to the **Motion Presets** folder inside the **Ch_4_Exercises** folder, and open **InviteStart.indd**. Resave the file as **InviteWorking.indd** in the same folder. If you want to see the finished file, open **InviteDone.indd** and preview it.

2. In the Layers panel, make sure the **Moon** layer is selected and unlocked. Select the Line tool ( ), and draw a diagonal line from the center of the blue moon to the upper-right corner of the page (**Figure 4.12**). Leave some room for the moon to grow larger as it rises.

Figure 4.12 Using the Line tool, start at the center of the moon, and drag up to the upper-right corner of the page. Don't go all the way to the corner; leave some room for the moon to grow larger.

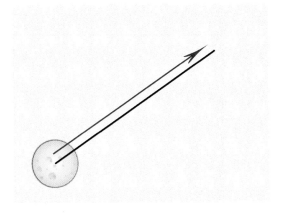

3. Now you'll convert the diagonal line to a motion path. Select both the path and the moon, and click the Convert to Motion Path icon ( ) at the bottom of the Animation panel. Use the following settings:

- **Event:** On Page Load

- **Duration:** 2 seconds

- **Speed:** Ease Out

- **Animate:** From Current Appearance

- **Animate Scale:** 150%

- **Visibility:** Hide Until Animated

These settings will hide the moon until it begins to rise and grow larger. If necessary, tweak the length and angle of the path—you have to allow for the increase in the diameter of the moon so it isn't cropped by the edge of the page.

4. Lock the **Moon** layer, and click the visibility control by the **Once in a Blue Moon** layer to make it visible. Select the layer to target it.

5. Using either the Pen or the Pencil tool, create a curved path that will bring the "Once in a Blue Moon" text in along a short counterclockwise arc (**Figure 4.13**). Start below the text, and end the curved path near the center of the text. You'll designate this path as a motion path after you choose the initial motion preset.

Figure 4.13 Create a short, counterclockwise arc to guide the blue text up to the top of the page.

6. In the Animation panel, choose the Fade In preset as a start, and use the following settings:

- **Event:** On Page Load
- **Duration:** 2.5 seconds
- **Speed:** From Preset
- **Animate:** To Current Location
- **Animate Scale:** 120%
- **Visibility:** Hide Until Animated

7. Select the arc path and the text (which have already been converted to outlines), and click the Convert to Motion Path icon at the bottom of the Animation panel.

8. The moon should start rising, followed by the appearance of the text. Use the Timing panel to control when each component plays. Select both animations in the Timing panel, and click the Play Together link at the bottom of the panel (**Figure 4.14**). (Ignore the existing animation in the Timing panel; it will make its appearance later in the exercise.) Preview the animation, save the file, and keep it open.

Figure 4.14 Synchronize the moonrise and the blue text so they play together.

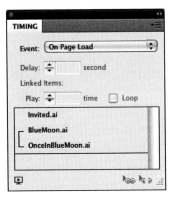

9. Now you'll create a motion path and save it as a custom preset that you can use for other objects. Hide the **Party**, **Once in a Blue Moon**, and **Moon** layers. Reveal the **Balloons** layer, and select it to target it. With the Pen or Pencil tool, create an S-shaped path that starts at the center of the green-and-purple balloon and stops short of the top of the page (**Figure 4.15**). You'll probably want to tweak the path after you test the animation; you want the balloon to float upward, but not off the page. Remember that the stroke attributes of the path aren't important; it becomes invisible once it's designated as a motion path.

Figure 4.15 Create an S-shaped path for the green-and-purple balloon to follow as it floats upward.

10. Select the balloon and the path, and click the Convert to Motion Path icon at the bottom of the Animation panel. Use the following settings:

    ▫ **Event:** On Page Load

    ▫ **Duration:** 3 seconds

    ▫ **Speed:** None

    ▫ **Animate:** From Current Appearance

    ▫ **Animate Scale:** 100%

    ▫ **Opacity:** Fade Out

11. To save the balloon motion as a motion preset, choose Save from the Animation panel menu. Name the motion preset **Balloon Float** in the Save Preset dialog (**Figure 4.16**) and click OK.

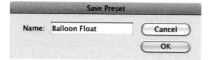

Figure 4.16 Name your new motion preset.

12. Now you'll apply the new custom motion preset to the other balloon. Select the purple-and-yellow balloon, and choose the **Balloon Float** preset in the Animation panel; notice that it's displayed in a separate part of the Preset pull-down menu, near the top. That's where your custom presets will appear. Examine the settings. Everything you specified for the first balloon has been stored in the preset, giving you a big head start on the second balloon. Change one thing: Set the Opacity to None, so the second balloon doesn't fade out.

13. Preview the animation. Reposition the purple-and-yellow balloon if it flies off the left side of the page. If you wish to edit the balloon's motion path, select the balloon, then switch to the white arrow and select the motion path. Once it's selected, you can move, add, or delete anchor points to change its travel. Such edits will not alter the custom motion preset you created—the changes will apply just to this balloon's animation.

14. It would be nice if the second balloon appeared in front of the text at the top of the invitation. In the Layers panel, turn the visibility of the **Once in a Blue Moon** layer back on, and unlock the layer. Select the purple-and-yellow balloon in the **Balloons** layer, and use the small blue target square in the **Balloons** layer to push the balloon up to the topmost layer (**Figure 4.17**).

Figure 4.17 Move the purple-and-yellow balloon up to the Once in a Blue Moon layer by pushing the blue target square up to the top layer.

15. Reveal the **Party** layer, and select the "We Have a Party" text. In the Animation panel, choose the Fade In preset and use the following settings:

- **Event:** On Page Load
- **Duration:** 3.5 seconds
- **Speed:** From Preset
- **Animate:** From Current Appearance
- **Animate Scale:** 200%
- **Opacity:** Fade In
- **Visibility:** Hide Until Animated

16. Finally, reveal all layers. The text in the **You're Invited** layer has already been animated. All you have to do is slightly rearrange the order in the Timing panel and link most of the animations together.

17. In the Timing panel, drag the **Invited.ai** animation to the bottom of the list. Drag **balloon.ai** and **balloon2.ai** up in the timing list so they're just below **BlueMoon.ai** (**Figure 4.18**). Select all of the animations except **Invited.ai**, and link them so they start together on page load. They have different durations, so they don't all finish simultaneously. Preview the animation, save the file, and keep it open.

Figure 4.18 Arrange the animations in the Timing panel as shown. Link all the animations except **Invited.ai**.

Exporting and Importing Motion Presets

Motion presets are not document-specific. When you save a preset, it becomes part of InDesign's arsenal for all documents. You should save the **Balloon Float** preset in case you ever need it again.

1. From the Animation panel menu, choose Manage Presets. Select the **Balloon Float** preset at the top of the list, and then click the Save As button. You can save motion presets anywhere; they're just XML files. Navigate to the **Motion Presets** folder inside the **Ch_4_Exercises** folder, name the preset **BalloonFloat.xml**, and click Save. You have to save presets one at a time, so if you want to store multiple custom presets, you'll have to export them like this, one by one. Keep the Manage Presets dialog open for the next step.

2. So you'll know how to import custom motion presets, you'll delete the **Balloon Float** preset and then re-import it. Select the **Balloon Float** preset and click the Delete button. InDesign warns you that there is no undo for this move (**Figure 4.19**); click OK.

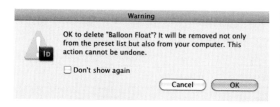

Figure 4.19 InDesign warns you that deleting a motion preset in the Manage Presets dialog cannot be undone.

3. Back in the Manage Presets dialog, click the Load button, navigate to the folder where you saved the **BalloonFloat.xml** file, select the file, and click Open. Although you must save presets one at a time, you can load multiple motion presets at once. Preview the file one last time, and tweak anything you'd like to change. You're finished with this exercise; you can close the file.

In this exercise, you played with a number of motion presets, learned how to create and use a motion path, and learned how to save and load custom motion presets. You should feel more familiar with the controls in the Animation panel and the wonderful selection of motion presets InDesign gives you. You should also be starting to get a sense of how you can combine durations and animation order in the Timing panel to make things happen when you want. And it's all pretty easy, isn't it?

Page Transitions

As the user navigates from page to page in your project, it's (usually) obvious to them that they're reading through a multipage document. If you provide buttons that lead them to the next page, they'll click on a "next page" button and the current page will be replaced by the next one (more about that in the next chapter). But if you'd like a fancier transition from one page to another, you might want to explore InDesign's built-in page transitions. You may have seen the default Page Curl (way too cute), but there are others.

NOTE: If the page curl effect isn't working in the Preview panel, choose Edit Preview Settings from the Preview panel menu, and make sure that the Include Interactive Page Curl option is checked. You may have to refresh the Preview panel by Alt/Option-clicking the play icon on the bottom of the panel.

1. In the **Page Transitions** folder inside the **Ch_4_Exercises** folder, open **Paintings.indd**. Resave the file as **PaintingsWorking.indd** in the same folder. Drag on the corner of the Preview panel so that you can more easily experiment with the default page curl, and set it to Preview Document mode (). If necessary, click the Play triangle in the bottom left corner of the Preview panel to render the document. Hover your cursor over the upper-right or lower-right corner of the cover page of the project, and you'll see the "paper" start to curl, much like a real magazine page. Hold down the mouse button and keep dragging toward the left side of the Preview window, and the experience is much like turning the page in a magazine printed on very thin paper (**Figure 4.20**). In fact, you may find it difficult to let go of the page in order to complete the transition to the next page— it's sort of like that scene in *National Lampoon's Christmas Vacation* when Chevy Chase is trying to read a magazine with pine sap on his hands. You'll be relieved to know that the experience is much better in the exported SWF.

Figure 4.20 The default SWF page curl is similar to turning pages in a printed magazine.

2. Launch your default Web browser, choose File > Open File, navigate to the **PaintingsExport** folder inside the **Page Transitions** folder, and open **Paintings.html**. Try turning the pages in your Web browser, and you should find that the page-turning behavior is much more natural. When you drag far enough toward the opposite side of the screen, the page should turn—and stay that way. Note that the page turn works whether you are paging forward or backward in the project, but only works when you click the corners, not on the straight edges of the page.

3. Return to InDesign so you can explore more page transition options. If you rely on the page curl to take a reader from page to page, you may find you don't need navigation buttons in a simple document. But you'll have to make sure they know to peel the pages by the corners, and that isn't obvious. You may decide that, however cute the page curl might be, you'd still like to provide buttons as a more obvious method of turning pages. But that doesn't mean you can't still entertain the user during the page-turning experience. It's time to experiment with page transitions. In the Layers panel, reveal the **Nav Buttons** layer; "next page" and "previous page" buttons have already been created for you.

4. In the Pages panel, select all seven page thumbnails. From the Pages panel menu, select Page Transitions > Choose to see the dozen page transition effects available (**Figure 4.21**). The examples themselves are animated; roll your cursor over one of the options to see the transition in action. Choose the Dissolve transition by clicking the radio button under its example, and click OK.

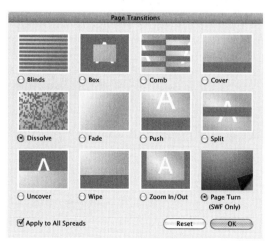

Figure 4.21 Page transition options. Roll over each option, and the example becomes animated to show you the effect. Note the option to apply to all spreads. All page transitions translate to interactive PDF except the Page Turn transition.

NOTE: During export to SWF, you're given the choice of using a Paper color or Transparent background. If you choose the Transparent option, all page transitions (including the page curl) are disabled. If your page transitions aren't working, export settings are the likely culprits.

5. If necessary, set the Preview panel to Preview Document mode. In the Preview panel menu, choose Edit Preview Settings and turn off the Include Interactive Page Curl option (**Figure 4.22**); the Page Curl option is on by default. Having the curl won't prevent your page transition effects from working, but the cumulative effect of the Dissolve transition, the page curl, and the navigation buttons would probably be sensory overload for a reader. As they attempted to click the navigation button for the next page, the page would unexpectedly curl, then dissolve... well, it would just be too much. There's something to be said for restraint.

Figure 4.22 To test page transitions, turn off the Include Interactive Page Curl option. Remember this option if you do want the page curl and wonder why it isn't working (the option is on by default).

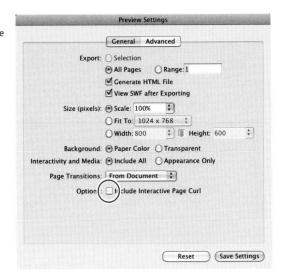

Click through the document in the Preview panel; what do you think of the Dissolve transition?

6. If the twelve page transitions aren't enough, you can customize the behavior of the transitions to shake things up (**Figure 4.23**). Open the Page Transitions panel (Window > Page Transitions), and select the Push transition. Click the Direction pull-down to see the options, and select the Right Up option. Click the Speed pull-down to see that you can choose from Slow, Medium, and Fast. Leave the Speed option at the default: Medium. Click the Apply to All Spreads icon in the lower-right corner of the panel, and check the results in the Preview panel.

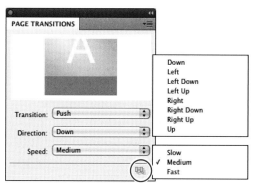

Figure 4.23 You can customize page transitions by changing the speed and direction. Click the Apply to All Spreads icon (circled) if you neglected to select all spreads beforehand.

Experiment with other transitions; edit them to see what works best for this document. You can even apply a different transition to each page. (Remember: just because you can, that doesn't mean you should. Control the urge.) Pages with a transition assigned will display a small icon in the Pages panel (**Figure 4.24**). You can also choose page transitions from Layout > Pages > Page Transitions > Choose (they just hide these little goodies everywhere, don't they?).

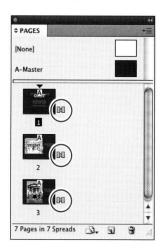

Figure 4.24 A small icon (circled) indicates which pages have been assigned page transitions.

7. Even if you pull on the corners of the Preview panel for a larger preview, you should still export to SWF and view the results in a browser for the full effect. What looks amusing in the Preview panel may prove to be overwhelming at full size in the final state. Decide on the page transition (or transitions) that you feel would be suitable for this small catalog of an artist's work, and choose File > Export. Choose Flash Player (SWF) for the format, and navigate to the folder named **Paintings (Your Version)** inside the Page Transitions folder. Name the SWF **Paintings.swf**. In the export dialog, use the following settings:

- **Generate HTML File:** This enables you to view directly in a browser.

- **View SWF after Exporting:** Automatically displays the SWF in your default browser.

- **Scale:** 100%

- **Background:** Paper Color—even though the project has a charcoal gray background; if you check Transparent, page transitions won't be included.

- **Page Transitions:** From Document, to preserve your choices. Note that you can select a transition from the pull-down menu, though, and override existing page transitions during export.

- **Options:** Uncheck the option to Include Interactive Page Curl.

8. Page through the Paintings project in your browser and see what you think. Do you like the transition (or transitions) you chose? Do the page transitions enhance the reader's experience, or do they compete for the reader's attention, detracting from the paintings, which are the central subjects? You might even decide to dispense with the fancy transitions after all, and just let the reader move sedately from page to page using the navigation buttons. It's up to you.

If you want to remove all page transitions and start over, select a page thumbnail (or multiple thumbnails) in the Pages panel and, from the panel menu, choose Page Transitions > Clear All. If you want to disable the page transition for a single page, the easiest way is to select the page thumbnail in the Pages panel, then right-click (Mac: Control-click) and choose Page Transitions > Clear Page Transition from the contextual menu.

TIP: Some of the animation effects may behave oddly when combined with a page transition—especially the page curl effect. You'll get your first hint in the Preview panel. As you page through the project in the Preview panel, if animations are not appearing, or are behaving unexpectedly, test the file by exporting to SWF and previewing in a browser. You may find that you have to dispense with either the animation or the assigned page transition. Some of the more common animation offenders are Fade In, Appear, Zoom in 2D, Swoosh, and the Fly-in presets. It's just One Of Those Things you'll have to consider as you start creating more adventurous projects. The easiest way to combat this problem is to make it a habit to rely on buttons to navigate to the next or previous page, disabling all transitions, and let your animation imagination run wild.

Chapter 5

Button Up

Buttons aren't just decorations (although they can be pretty cute); they really make things happen in your interactive projects. Buttons can trigger animations, jump from page to page in a project, and create rollover effects. They can provide precise control over events, and they can provide visible hints to the reader to *click here* to make something happen.

Buttons in interactive documents are very much like real-life buttons: They're intended to trigger an action that is already available, such as turning a device on or off. In some cases, though, you can create a button in anticipation of its use, such as a button with a "next page" action attached, even though you haven't yet created all the pages of the document. But in any case, a button acts on something else. A video plays whether it's triggered by a separate button, or by directly clicking the video. The button needs a video to trigger; you might think of the button as part of a partnership.

In this chapter, we'll first look at the button triggers that make something happen (and all the events buttons can trigger), and then you'll explore the ways you can control the appearance of buttons.

Button Events

Buttons have six active behaviors (which InDesign calls "events") that can act as triggers for actions. Since two of those behaviors work only in exported PDFs, we'll concentrate on using the four events that work as triggers in exported SWF files:

- **On Release.** This is the instant the user releases the mouse button after clicking, and it's when users expect something to happen. This is the most commonly used trigger.

- **On Click.** This is the bottom of a click, and it's usually a bit premature to be used as a trigger, since it will usually catch users by surprise.

- **On Roll Over.** The button area is actually a hot spot. You can trigger events by just moving your cursor over the button area. This is usually used to trigger remote rollover events, such as causing a graphic to appear or prompting an animation to play.

- **On Roll Off.** This is the moment when your cursor leaves the hot spot area of the button. This option is usually used in tandem with the On Roll Over trigger to hide a graphic that was revealed by On Roll Over.

For the record, here are the button events that only work in PDFs (all events described above work in both SWF and PDF export):

- **On Focus.** This is similar to the On Roll Over event, but is usually accomplished by tabbing from another field into the button area. This is sometimes used in Acrobat forms to trigger an event as the user tabs through the fields in the form. The On Focus moment occurs when the tabbing lands the focus on the target button area.

- **On Blur.** Similar to On Roll Off, this is the moment when a user tabs away from the button (again, usually in an Acrobat form).

Note that neither On Focus nor On Blur works in SWF export, so save them for documents that will be exported to interactive PDF.

Button States

Up. Down. Rollover. Button states sound a bit like dog tricks, don't they? In fact, button states are very similar to dog tricks. Let's compare:

Trick	Dog	Button
Up	■	■
Down	■	■
Rollover	■	■
Fetch	■	
Play Animation		■

As you can see, each has its advantages. While a dog can fetch, a button can trigger an animation (and, as an added bonus, buttons don't shed). A button's default state is labeled *Normal,* while its down state is referred to as *Click* by InDesign. (Acrobat refers to the default state as *Up.*)

It might be helpful to explore a simple file showing the On Release, On Click, On Roll Over, and On Roll Off events. If you haven't already copied the **Ch_5_Exercises** folder from the tutorial disc, do so now.

1. Navigate to the **Ch_5_Exercises** folder, and then to the **ButtonTriggers** folder. Launch a Web browser and open the file **ButtonTriggers.html** (or, if you have Adobe Media Player, launch it and view the **ButtonTriggers.swf** file directly).

2. Click the red capsule-shaped button at the top of the file. When you release the mouse button at the end of the click, a picture appears to the right of the button. This is what users expect, and On Release is the trigger you'll use most often.

3. Click the blue button. When you've fully pressed the mouse button down (but before you've released it), the picture disappears. The On Click trigger seems a bit sudden, doesn't it? Consequently, you may find that you rarely use the On Click trigger.

4. Roll your mouse over the red shirt button at the bottom, and you'll notice several things. First, the artwork isn't a dull standard button; it was created in Illustrator to look like a real-life shirt button. As you mouse over the button, it changes color and shows a green glow. The mouseover causes the image of a lion sculpture to appear, and mousing away from the button causes the image to disappear. This is because the button has separate actions attached to the Roll Over and Roll Off states.

5. Now you'll examine the InDesign file that created the **ButtonTriggers.swf** file that you've been viewing. Close the Web browser or Adobe Media Player and, if necessary, launch InDesign CS5. In the **ButtonTriggers** folder, open **ButtonTriggers.indd**. This is the InDesign file that generated the SWF file. You'll explore the InDesign file to see how the buttons were set up. Later in this chapter you'll create your own buttons. Save the file as **ButtonTriggersWorking.indd** in the **ButtonTriggers** folder.

6. Open the Buttons panel (Window > Interactive > Buttons). Select the red button at the top of the page with the Selection tool (black arrow), and examine the settings in the Buttons panel (**Figure 5.1**).

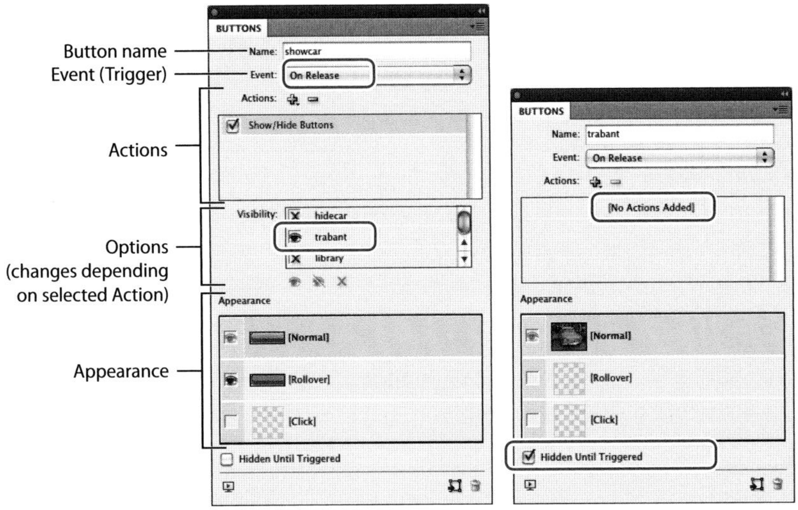

Figure 5.1 The Buttons panel tells the story. The **showcar** button (left) displays the **trabant** button when the user clicks and releases the mouse button. The **trabant** button (right) just contains the image of an automobile, and is set to be hidden until triggered.

■ **Event.** The On Release option means that the requested action is triggered at the moment the user releases the mouse button (at the end of a click).

▫ **Action.** The Show/Hide action is used to show the picture of the automobile. The target of the action is another button (**trabant**), whose sole purpose is to hold the automobile image and hide until triggered.

▫ **Appearance.** A button can have three separate appearances: Normal, Rollover, and Click. This button has two appearances, but you won't notice the Rollover appearance unless you roll over it. If you like, click the Preview icon (⬛) at the bottom of the Buttons panel, and try rolling over the red button in the Preview panel. By the way, the button artwork is one of the prefab buttons that ships with InDesign CS5; we'll explore those later.

7. Select the frame containing the automobile image. It's a button, too, named **trabant**. (The Trabant was a small car that was produced in East Germany between 1957 and 1991, if you're curious.) Check the settings in the Buttons panel. The button has no attached actions; it's just there to hold the automobile image, and it's hidden until triggered by the **showcar** button.

Let's sum up the relationship between the red button and the automobile image. The automobile button containing the image is hidden until the user clicks the red button, which triggers a Show/Hide Buttons action that makes the automobile button visible. The Show/Hide Buttons action, as its name implies, only operates on buttons, so it can't be used to display or hide other objects.

Now you'll examine the blue button that you clicked to hide the Trabant image; it also has a Show/Hide relationship with the **trabant** button. Select the blue button (in the page, not in the Preview panel) and examine its settings in the Buttons panel (**Figure 5.2**).

▫ **Event.** The On Click option means that the requested action is triggered at the moment the user's mouse button reaches the bottom of travel.

▫ **Action.** The Show/Hide action is used to hide the **trabant** button containing the picture of the automobile. More than one action can be assigned to a button.

▫ **Appearance.** This is another one of the buttons that ship with InDesign. The button artwork contains two appearances: Normal and Rollover. If you like, click the Preview icon in the Buttons panel to test the Rollover state in the Preview panel. It's subtle, but keep it in mind; visual feedback, such as a change in button appearance, can keep the user engaged and informed.

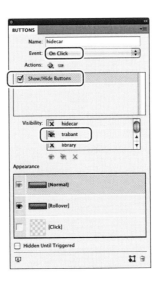

Figure 5.2 A Show/Hide Buttons action can be assigned to any button event. Here, it's assigned to the On Click event.

Finally, you'll examine the "shirt button" at the bottom of the page, which has a more complex appearance. You'll explore how that was accomplished, and you'll add a third appearance, for the Click event. A button's appearance can come from a placed graphic, modifications to the fill and stroke attributes, manipulations of InDesign effects (such as shadows and glows) applied to the object—or a combination of all of those influences, if you get really carried away. You can even place three different graphics into a button: one for each appearance. How is this possible in a single frame? It isn't exactly a single frame; a button is a special object with multiple *states*, each of which can have a different appearance and function. You might think of a button as a sort of "hot spot" with a storage bin.

1. Select the shirt button in the page, look in the Buttons panel, and note that the button has two very different appearances. In its Normal state (its appearance before it's clicked), it's a red button. In its Rollover state, it's green and has a green glow (**Figure 5.3**).

2. With the Direct Selection tool (white arrow), select the shirt button in the page. Choose the Normal appearance in the Buttons panel. Choose Object > Object Layer Options to find out what's going on in this state. The button artwork is an Adobe Illustrator file with three layers. For the Normal state, only the **RedNoGlow** layer is visible (**Figure 5.4**). While separate artwork files could be used for the button states, it's easier to keep track of just one file, and let InDesign's Object Layer Options control the layer visibility. This approach will work with Illustrator (.ai) files, Photoshop (.psd) files, and layered PDFs. Object Layer Options have no effect on the state of the saved file; they just control layer visibility within InDesign.

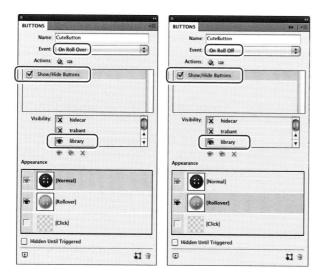

Figure 5.3
The "shirt button" changes color and glows in its Rollover state, thanks to a combination of Object Layer Options and InDesign effects.

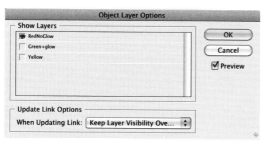

Figure 5.4 Only the **RedNoGlow** layer is visible in the placed Adobe Illustrator file when the button is in the Normal state.

3. In the Buttons panel, select the Rollover state in the Appearance section. The button is green in this state because of a different choice in the Object Layer Options, but notice what happens when you attempt to choose Object > Object Layer Options—you can't! Deselect the button, and then reselect it with the Direct Selection tool (you have to sort of sneak up on it…). Now that you're addressing the graphic directly, you'll be able to access the Object Layer Options dialog to see that the **Green+glow** layer is set to be the only visible layer (**Figure 5.5**).

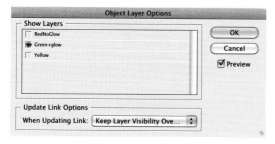

Figure 5.5 The Rollover state of the button reveals only the **Green+glow** layer in the Illustrator file, and hides the other layers.

Now you'll decorate the third state of the button with another appearance, still using the same placed Illustrator file and InDesign's Object Layer Options. If necessary, reselect the button in the page, and then select the Click state in the Buttons panel to activate it. Initially, it displays the button artwork in red (since it's invoking the saved state of the Illustrator file). Hover over the Content Grabber "viewfinder" icon (⊚) in the center of the image, and click to select the image. Now you can use Object Layer Options to turn off the **RedNoGlow** and **Green+glow** layers, and turn on the **Yellow** layer (**Figure 5.6**). Why did you have to select the graphic directly to control layer visibility? Well, once a button develops more than one state, it's ceased to be a simple frame, and is now a multistate object; you have to select the image inside, rather than the container, to use Object Layer Options. You won't be assigning another action to this state; it's just for amusing visual feedback when the user clicks. Test the button in the Preview panel. It's certainly colorful, isn't it? Save and close the file.

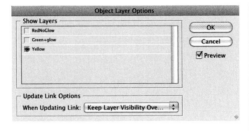

Figure 5.6 Activate the Click state in the Buttons panel, and use Object Layer Options to turn on the visibility of the **Yellow** layer in the Illustrator file decorating the button.

Button Appearance

You don't have to create fancy artwork such as the shirt button in the preceding exercise, but isn't it cool that you can use a variety of graphics to decorate your buttons? You can have attractive buttons even if you don't feel like creating original artwork in Photoshop or Illustrator; InDesign provides a nice starter kit for you. Let's explore the possibilities.

Sample Buttons in InDesign

To view the freebie InDesign buttons, go to the Buttons panel menu and choose Sample Buttons. What you'll see is actually an InDesign library (**Figure 5.7**) containing 52 separate buttons, all with built-in actions attached. (You can change these actions if you like; more on that later.)

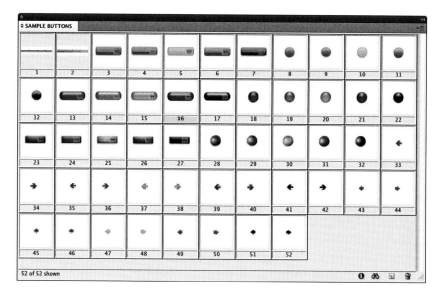

TIP: If you haven't used InDesign libraries before, they're just a repository of page geometry. That's Latin for "kind of like a big Clipboard you can store lots of stuff in." Any object you've created in an InDesign document can be dragged into a library. Libraries are not document-specific, so their contents can be made available for any document.

Figure 5.7 InDesign's Sample Buttons library: one for every week of the year.

The buttons are simply numbered 1 through 52, which gives no hint of the actions already wired into them. You might find this list helpful:

- **Buttons 1 and 2.** These two library entries consist of multiple buttons arranged to look like navigational bars. Once you ungroup and select them, you'll find that they all use the Go To Page action. Since they're generic buttons, you would have to fill in the blanks and specify a target in the document for each button. And here's a general caveat: While the Go To Page action works in exported SWF files, it does nothing in an exported PDF. InDesign is nothing if not polite; at least you're warned about this if you attempt to export a PDF from a file containing buttons with Go To Page actions attached.

- **Buttons 3-12.** All of these buttons have been assigned **Go To URL** actions, which can take the user to Web addresses, or can incorporate an e-mail address to trigger an e-mail application (by using the "mailto" format). The Go To URL actions work in both SWF and PDF export.

- **Buttons 13-22.** Go To Page.

- **Buttons 23-32.** Go To URL.

- **Buttons 33-51 (odd numbers).** Notice that the odd-numbered buttons are all left-pointing, which gives a hint about their function: They all use the Go To Previous Page action, which works in both SWF and PDF export.

- **Buttons 34-52 (even numbers).** All right-pointing, even-numbered buttons in this range use the Go To Next Page action.

To use one of the sample buttons, just drag it into the document. If you drag a button from the Sample Buttons library, it determines the highest-numbered button in the document, adds 2, and then names itself. For example, if there's a Button 27 in the document, dragging a sample button onto the page will create Button 29. If you duplicate an existing button by Alt/Option-dragging, the new button's number is incremented by 2. For example, if you Alt/Option-drag to duplicate Button 6, the duplicate names itself Button 8, and if you Alt/Option-drag Button 13, its duplicate names itself Button 15. Buttons that you create from existing objects name themselves Button 1, Button 2, Button 3, and so on. Of course, you can rename a button in the Buttons panel and modify its function. Let's do a little experiment to see how the sample buttons behave.

1. Start with a new, blank Web document. Choose File > New > Document. For Intent, choose Web, set the number of pages to 4, and select the 640 px x 480 px option from the Page Size pull-down menu (**Figure 5.8**). This won't be much of a design; it's just a place for playing with buttons. Save the file as **ButtonWork.indd** in the **Ch_5_Exercises** folder and leave the file open.

Figure 5.8 Create a simple, four-page Web document for button experimentation.

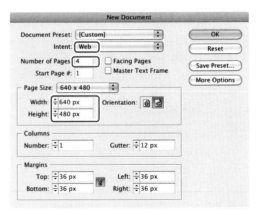

2. Since you'll be trying out the Go To Page action, it will be helpful if your document has page numbers for identification (so you can tell if you've actually gone to a page). To make it easy, you'll create automatic page numbers on the master page. Double-click the A-Master icon in the Pages panel. Using the Type tool, create a small text frame in the bottom margin. Type **Page,** press the spacebar, and then choose Type > Insert Special Character > Markers > Current Page Number (or, if you're using a two-button mouse, just right-click in the text frame and choose Insert Special Character > Markers > Current Page Number). Since you're on the master page, you'll just see "A" representing the page number (**Figure 5.9**). Select the text and set it to 20 px in size.

3. Double-click the icon for page 1 in the Pages panel. If necessary, open the Sample Buttons library from the Buttons panel menu. You can dock the library with other panels if you like. Drag Button 16 (a red capsule-shaped button) onto the page, and take a look at its settings in the Buttons panel. It's named itself **Button 2**, and has two states (Normal and Rollover), each with its own appearance (**Figure 5.10**). Click the Rollover state in the Buttons panel to see what makes it different from the Normal state; the Rollover state has a gray glow around it. Even though the button is set to perform its Go To Page action only when clicked (not during a rollover), the visual change during rollover can be a subtle hint to the user that the button is "alive," and such feedback is a nice way to engage the user.

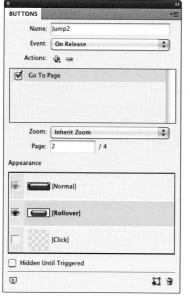

Figure 5.9 Automatic page number on a master page.

Figure 5.10 This sample InDesign button has two distinct appearances. A gray glow appears in the Rollover state.

4. Change the name of the button to **Jump2**, and enter **2** in the Page field to specify which page the user will see after clicking the button. Change the mode of the Preview panel to Preview Document mode (see Chapter 2 if you don't remember how to do this), and then test the behavior of the button in the Preview panel. Does it take you to page 2 of the document? (You may have to enlarge the Preview panel so the page numbers are legible.) If clicking the button in the Preview panel doesn't take you to page 2, go back to page 1 in the document, select the button, and check your settings.

5. Take a look at the button in the page, and note the heavy dashed border around it, indicating that it's a button (it's a much coarser and heavier border than you see around object groups). Under the hood, this button is fairly complex. How hard would it be for you to create such a button in Illustrator? Take a look at similar artwork deconstructed in Illustrator (**Figure 5.11**). It involves all manner of embedded images and clipping masks. Yikes! It gives you some appreciation for the head start you've been given with the sample buttons, doesn't it?

Figure 5.11 One of InDesign's sample buttons, in Illustrator's exploded view. Think of all the work you don't have to do.

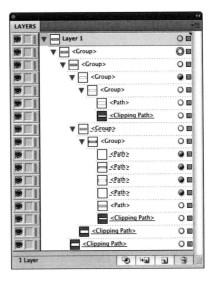

6. If necessary, navigate back to page 1 of the document. Drag the **5** button from the Sample Buttons library into the page. In the Buttons panel, note that this button has a Go To URL action built in, so change the button name to **URL**, and in the URL field, complete the Web address so it reads **http://www.adobe.com**. Test the URL button in the Preview panel. It should launch your default Web browser and take you to the Adobe Web

site. (You may have to click the Play button in the Preview panel to refresh the preview, and then click the green button again.)

7. Save the file, and keep it open for the next section (or take a break and eat a Twinkie).

What's the Twinkie® Finger?*

Each button sports an icon identifying it as a button, lest you mistake it for just an ordinary page object. It's a finger pressing a button, but ever since a student in one of my classes asked "What's the Twinkie finger?" I've been unable to think of it without thinking of Twinkies. And now I'm passing that on to you.

*Apologies to Hostess Brands, Inc.

Any Frame Can Be a Button

What if you've used all 52 buttons but yearn for more? You'll be excited to discover that any frame created in InDesign can become a button, whether it began life as a text frame, a graphics frame, or an unassigned frame. (Note, however, that frames containing video or audio cannot be converted to buttons— although, of course, they can be triggered by buttons.) Now you'll convert a text frame to a button to see how easy it is.

1. Navigate to page 2 of the document. With the Type tool, click and drag to create a text frame 150 px wide by 40 px tall. Type **Page 3** in the frame, and center the text both vertically and horizontally in the frame. There are multiple methods for accomplishing the horizontal centering; the easiest way is to use a keyboard shortcut (Mac: Cmd-Shift-C, Windows: Ctrl-Shift-C). To vertically center the type, press the Esc key to switch to the Selection tool so the frame (rather than the text) is selected. Then, choose Object > Text Frame Options and choose the Center option for vertical alignment (or use the Control panel options).

2. Fill the frame with the RGB Red swatch, and change the text color to Paper. Set the text to Myriad Pro Bold, 20 px.

3. Select the frame, right-click, and choose Effects > Bevel and Emboss (**Figure 5.12**). (Mac users without a two-button mouse can hold down the Control key to mimic having a right mouse button, while clicking to view the contextual menu.) Use the settings described below, and then click OK.

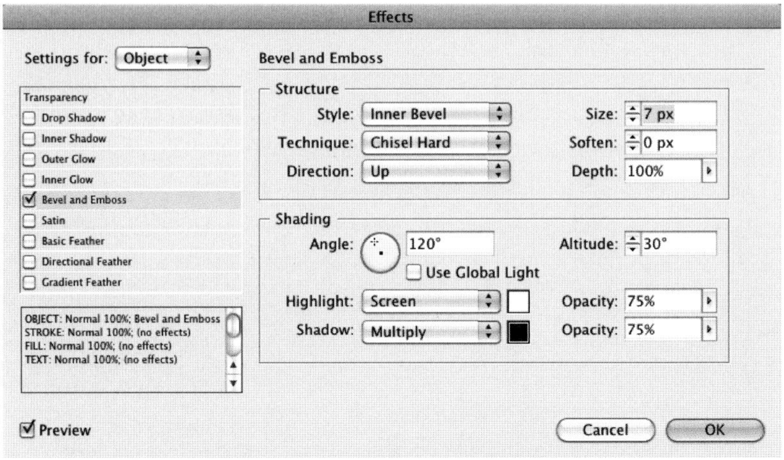

Figure 5.12 Adding a Bevel and Emboss effect to a frame is a quick way to create a button appearance.

Use the following settings (and leave the remaining options at the default):

- **Style:** Inner Bevel
- **Size:** 7 px
- **Technique:** Chisel Hard
- **Direction:** Up

4. It looks like a button, but it isn't truly a button until you click the Convert to Button icon (🔲) at the bottom of the Buttons panel. (Alternatively, if you're using a two-button mouse, you can right-click and choose Interactive > Convert to Button from the contextual menu.)

5. Name the new button **Page3**, leave the Event option at the default (On Release), and click the plus sign next to the Actions label. Choose the Go To Next Page action (you could also use the Go To Page action and set the target to page 3; both methods achieve the same result). If necessary, set the Preview panel to Preview Document mode and test the button. Navigate back to page 2 for the next step (you can use the small back/forward page controls at the bottom of the Preview panel), and save the file.

6. Now you'll see how easy it is to create an alternate appearance for a new button state. If necessary, reselect the button and then click the Rollover state in the Buttons panel. That's all it takes to create a new state, but currently the Rollover state looks no different from the Normal state. With the button still selected, choose the RGB Green swatch in the Swatches panel. Test the button in the Preview panel and make sure it turns bright green when you roll over it.

TIP: Since you'll check your document frequently in the Preview panel, here are some handy keyboard shortcuts:

Preview Spread: Cmd-Shift-Return (Mac); Ctrl-Shift-Enter (Windows)

Preview Document: Cmd-Opt-Shift-Return (Mac); Ctrl-Alt-Shift-Enter (Windows)

7. But wait—there's more. Make sure the Rollover state is still selected in the Buttons panel, and then right-click (Mac: Control-click) the button in the document and choose Effects > Outer Glow from the contextual menu. Click the small square to the right of the blending mode pull-down menu, and choose RGB Green. Set the blending mode to Normal (**Figure 5.13**). While you're in the dialog, notice that InDesign describes the selected button as a group; while it's treated as a single object when you select it in the page, InDesign regards it as sort of an assembly of one red and one green frame. It's crazy, but it works. Test the button by rolling over it in the Preview panel (you may have to refresh the preview and enlarge the Preview panel to clearly see the glow effect). Save the file and keep it open for the next section (or take a break and have another Twinkie).

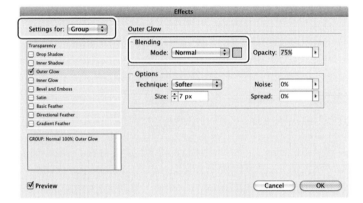

Figure 5.13 Adding a glow to a button state appearance. Note that InDesign regards the single button as a group.

Changing Content in a Button State

As you saw in the earlier Button Triggers exercise, InDesign's Object Layer Options can be used to control the visibility of layers in a multilayer Illustrator file. The same trick can be used with multilayer Photoshop files or PDFs. But you can also place separate files into a button's states, or change text between states.

1. Navigate to page 3 of the **ButtonWork.indd** document. Choose File > Place, navigate to the **VariableButtons** folder in the **Ch_5_Exercises** folder, and select **ButtonBase.ai**. IMPORTANT: Hold down the Shift key as you click the Open button in the Place dialog to launch the Place dialog (**Figure 5.14**). In the dialog, choose Crop to Media and click OK. This is to ensure that InDesign creates a frame to the same dimensions as the Illustrator file's artboard (rather than cropping to the artwork), which will allow room for other artwork you're going to use in the button. (You might

have noticed that the title bar of the dialog reads "Place PDF"—this is because native Illustrator files are actually PDFs inside.) Click in the page to
place the button graphic.

Figure 5.14 Set the
ButtonBase.ai crop to
Media to allow room for
artwork to be used in
other states of the button.

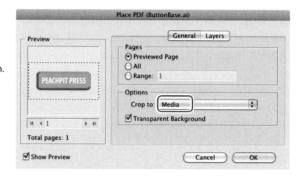

2. Right-click on the frame and choose Interactive > Convert to Button from
   the contextual menu, or choose Window > Interactive > Buttons. The
   Buttons panel appears. Name the button **Peachpit**.

3. Click the Rollover state in the Buttons panel to make it active. You're going
   to place a Photoshop file into the button in the Rollover state to change its
   appearance. To do this, you have to "reach inside" the button to place the
   new artwork. If you have the button selected with the Selection tool (black
   arrow), a new frame will be created when you place the new graphic. So,
   either click the Content Grabber (the viewfinder-like icon in the middle
   of the button as you hover over it) or switch to the Direct Selection tool
   (white arrow) and click inside the button. Either method selects the
   graphic so you can replace it in the Rollover state. Don't worry; it won't
   be deleted from the Normal state. You might think of the button states as
   separate containers within the button. With the Rollover state selected,
   choose File > Place, navigate to the **VariableButtons** folder again, and
   select **LeftBloop.psd**. There's no need to hold down Shift this time; just
   click OK.

4. Now you'll populate the Click state with another image. Click the Click
   state in the Buttons panel to activate it, and then select the **Peachpit**
   button by clicking inside it with the Direct Selection tool or by clicking
   the Content Grabber viewfinder icon. Choose File > Place, navigate to
   the **VariableButtons** folder one more time, and select **RightBloop.psd**.
   Without holding down the Shift key, click the OK button.

5. It's time to add an action to the button. In the Buttons panel, select the
   Normal state of the button just to restore it to that appearance. Click the

plus sign next to the Actions label, and then select the Go To URL action. In the URL field that appears once you've chosen the action, enter the complete URL: **http://www.peachpit.com**—InDesign thoughtfully enters the "http://" part for you. (Notice that there's also a minus sign next to the Action label, in case you ever wish to delete an existing action.) Refresh the Preview panel if necessary, and test the button. Note how it changes appearance when you roll over it, and again when you click it. When you click the button in the Preview panel, it should launch your default Web browser and take you to the Peachpit Press Web site.

6. Open the Links panel (Window > Links) and note that each button-state graphic is listed there (**Figure 5.15**). Since you placed the graphics, you'd expect them to appear in the Links panel, but you'll see that even though InDesign regards the button as a single entity, each state within the button is a separate component. Save the file and keep it open for the last part of the exercise.

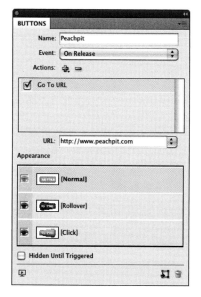

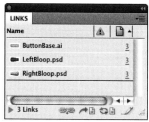

Figure 5.15 Three separate graphics are associated with the button. Each graphic populates a separate state of the button. You might think of it as three graphics frames within a single carrier.

As you saw on page 2 of your working file, you don't need to have any graphics files to decorate buttons; you can just start with a text frame and create a simple button by using fill and stroke attributes, with some beveling and embossing effects thrown in. But now that you're starting to realize that each state of a button can be addressed separately, you understand that there are lots of interesting things you can do to a button. There *are* some limitations, however: You cannot put multimedia content in a button state, and you cannot delete or disable the Normal button state. If you change the dimensions of one state of a button, it doesn't resize the contents in other states, but the hot spot area of the button is determined by the largest bounding box of the button. For example, if two button states are 2 inches wide by 1 inch high, but the third state is 3 inches wide by 2 inches high, the entire button area will be equivalent to the 3-inches-by-2-inches state.

The entire area of a button might not be filled (if, for example, it contains a small graphic), but the entire area is clickable. You should keep this in mind when you have several buttons close together, so that users don't accidentally click on the wrong button. You can also create buttons with no fill or stroke, so that they aren't visible, but can still be used as a hot spot to trigger actions.

7. Now you'll experiment with a button that's based on a text frame. Go to page 4 of the document and create a text frame using the following settings:

   - **Dimensions:** 250 px W, 50 px H

   - **Fill:** RGB Yellow, 100%

   - **Stroke:** 2 px Black

   - **Text Attributes:** Myriad Pro Bold, 28 px

8. Type **GO TO...** in all caps in the text frame. Center the text horizontally with the keyboard shortcut (Mac: Cmd-Shift-C, Windows: Ctrl-Shift-C). You can also use the alignment options in the Control panel. Choose Object > Text Frame Options and vertically center the text (you can also accomplish this in the Control panel).

9. Convert the text frame to a button by one of the methods you've learned. Name the button **firstpage**, and assign the Go To First Page action to the On Release event.

10. Select the Rollover state in the Buttons panel to activate it. Select the text in the button and change it to **FIRST PAGE**. Select the button with the Selection tool (or you can just press the Esc key to switch tools and select the button), and change the fill color to the RGB Cyan swatch.

11. Now you'll change the shape of the button. You can use the spiffy new Live Corner controls to quickly and easily change the appearance of the button (**Figure 5.16**). Click the small yellow square on the right side of the button frame. Yellow diamonds appear on the frame's corners. Drag one of the yellow diamonds toward the midpoint of one of the sides to round off all

the corners. If you want to be more adventurous, Alt/Option-click one of the diamonds to choose another corner option. Keep Alt/Option-clicking to cycle through the options. If you want to apply a corner style to just one corner, hold down Alt/Option-Shift and click the diamond to cycle through the styles for just that corner. Hold down the Shift key while dragging the corner control to affect the size of just that corner. The possibilities are endless (and potentially ugly).

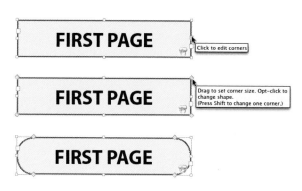

Figure 5.16 Click the small yellow square on the right side of the frame to activate Live Corners. Click one of the corners and drag it toward the midpoint of the frame to make all corners round. Here's the end result.

12. Select the Click state in the Buttons panel to activate it. Notice that the appearance of the Normal state is replicated in the Click state initially. Change the fill color to the RGB Green swatch, and delete the text inside the frame.

13. Make sure the center point of the Transform Proxy in the Control panel is selected (▦). Using the dimension fields in the Control panel, change both the width and height of the button to 52 px. Then, choose Object > Convert Shape > Ellipse to create a circle.

14. Set the Preview panel to Preview Document mode and test the button. You might have to refresh the panel by Alt/Option-clicking the Play button in the panel. Admittedly, these aren't the most elegant buttons, but they prove that there are many ways to modify the appearance of buttons without a lot of work. Save the file if you like, and close it. If you wish, you can quit InDesign for now; you'll be playing in Illustrator for a while.

Creating Button Art in Illustrator

Don't feel like being creative? Let Adobe Illustrator do the heavy lifting for you. Illustrator's built-in graphic styles make it easy to construct professional-looking buttons from shapes you create. If you're not even up to creating simple objects, take advantage of the prebuilt buttons available as symbols. And, as you saw with the cute little "shirt button" art in the first exercise in this chapter, the ability to use InDesign's Object Layer Options to control the visibility of layers in a placed Illustrator file expands the flexibility of Illustrator artwork. It's time to play!

Using Graphic Styles

A graphic style is a recipe for the appearance of an object in Illustrator. It can contain just a simple fill and stroke, or elaborate combinations of effects that can add glows, shadows, distortions, or patterns. You'll use some of Illustrator's built-in graphic styles that are geared specifically toward creating buttons.

1. Launch Adobe Illustrator CS4 or CS5; the options for button creation are the same in both versions. (If you have Illustrator CS3, the concepts and assortment of graphic styles are the same, but the selection of prebuilt buttons is completely different from CS4/CS5.) The illustrations in this chapter are from Illustrator CS5, but you shouldn't feel disoriented if you're using an earlier version.

2. Choose File > New and create a new document based on the Web Document Profile. This sets the document color mode to RGB and the resolution for raster effects to 72 ppi. Set the document dimensions to 288 px wide by 144 px high (**Figure 5.17**). (Even though the document color mode is RGB, you can specify colors in any color mode if you like. However, the color will be rendered in RGB.) Save the file as **ButtonStyles.ai** in the **IllustratorBasicButtons** folder inside the **Ch_5_Exercises** folder.

Figure 5.17 Create a new Illustrator document based on the Web Document Profile.

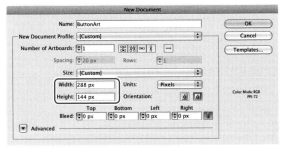

3. Press the **D** key on the keyboard (for "default") to set your fill and stroke attributes to the default opaque-white fill and 1-point black stroke. Choose the Rounded Rectangle tool from the Tool panel (it's hidden under the regular rectangle tool), and click anywhere in the page. This triggers the Rounded Rectangle Options dialog, which allows you to numerically

specify the dimensions and rounded corner radius. Set the values to 150 px wide, 75 px high, with a 15 px radius (**Figure 5.18**).

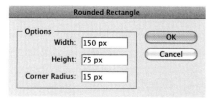

Figure 5.18 Choose the Rounded Rectangle tool, click in the page, and use these settings.

4. Switch to the Selection tool (black arrow), select the rounded rectangle, and position it approximately in the center of the artboard. It's pretty dull as buttons go, but you'll soon spruce it up by using graphic styles. Choose Window > Graphic Styles to open the basic set of styles. The starter kit of styles is pretty sparse, but Illustrator ships with more than just these few styles. From the Graphic Styles panel menu (that same little triangle-and-lines icon you see in the upper-right corner of every panel), choose Open Graphic Style Library > Buttons and Rollovers. Now you have something to work with (**Figure 5.19**).

Figure 5.19 Illustrator's Buttons and Rollovers graphic styles (with panel menu circled).

5. Hover over some of the styles and note the names: Bevel Red Normal, Bevel Red Mouse Down. Clearly, Illustrator is trying to give you a head start. If necessary, reselect the bland, boring button you created and try out some of the styles. With a single click, you can transform your rounded rectangle into an instant button. After experimenting with several of the styles, you'll notice that Illustrator has added each style you've tried to the main Graphic Styles panel.

6. From the panel menu of the Buttons and Rollovers graphic styles panel, choose Small List View so you can identify the styles more easily by their names. Apply the Opal Inlay Mouse Down style to your button, but don't close the Buttons and Rollovers panel yet; you need one more style to complete your button.

7. Open the Layers panel (Window > Layers) and double-click the Layer 1 name to open the Layer Options dialog. Change the name of the layer to **Down** and click OK.

8. From the Layers panel menu, choose Duplicate Down to create **Down Copy**. Double-click the **Down Copy** layer and change its name to **Normal**.

9. Select the button in the **Normal** layer, and apply the Opal Inlay Normal graphic style to it. To compare the two button states, turn off the visibility of the **Normal** layer. (By the way, it's your button; if you'd prefer to use another pair of graphic styles for the button's two states, feel free to do so.) Save the file.

10. If you'd like to test the button in InDesign, launch InDesign and create a quick document. From the Intent pull-down menu, choose Web, and from the Page Size pull-down, choose the default 800 x 600 pixel dimensions.

11. Choose File > Place, select **ButtonStyles.ai**, and hold down the Shift key as you click OK in the Place dialog so you can control the import options. In the Import Options dialog, choose Bounding Box (All Layers) for the Crop option (**Figure 5.20**). This option ensures that the button is just big enough to contain all artwork that constitutes the button, but no bigger than necessary. You may want to resize the button, as it's rather huge (I scaled it down to 25%).

Figure 5.20 The Bounding Box (All Layers) option ensures that the button is the optimum size. Not too big, not too small—just right (like Goldilocks).

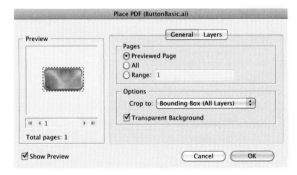

12. Convert the object to a button using one of the methods you've learned. In the Buttons panel, choose the Click state, select the graphic either with the Content Grabber or the Direct Selection tool, and then choose Object > Object Layer Options. In the Object Layer Options dialog, turn off the visibility of the **Normal** layer, leaving only the **Down** layer visible. Test the button in the Preview panel. You can add an action to the button's

On Release event if you wish, but that's not necessary to test the visual changes you've created.

13. Think about how little work you had to perform. Illustrator makes it almost painless to create attractive buttons. And, of course, you're not limited to the canned graphic styles; you can apply all manner of fill, stroke, and effects attributes to an object and save its appearance as a custom graphic style. Save and close the file.

Using Prebuilt Button Symbols

Don't feel like going to all the trouble of clicking and dragging to create a basic button, then applying a graphic style? Then you might enjoy the nice assortment of Web button art supplied with Illustrator as symbols.

About Symbols

Symbols are a special type of artwork. They're often used when a designer needs multiple instances of an object—for example, a school of fish based on an elaborate drawing of a fish consisting of multiple objects grouped together (body, fins, eyes, tail...). Copying that one fish 40 times could add substantially to file size, especially if the fish uses effects such as glows, shadows, and transparency. However, if the designer converts that one fish into a symbol (by dragging the original fish into the Symbols panel and giving it a name), adding 40 instances of the symbol doesn't increase the overhead in the file as much as 40 copies would. Symbols offer other advantages: If you edit the original symbol art, all the instances of the symbol reflect the changes. The Web buttons are supplied as symbols just as a convenience; in this case, the Symbols panel acts as sort of a repository (similar to a library in InDesign).

1. Create a new Illustrator document based on the Web document profile, and use the 640 px wide by 480 px high preset size. Save the file as **MultiButtons.ai** in the **Ch_5_Exercises** folder.

2. Open the Symbols panel (Window > Symbols). Since your document is based on the Web document profile, Illustrator automatically populates the panel with a few Web-appropriate symbols (**Figure 5.21**). (If you see a different set of symbols, it may be because you inadvertently chose the Print document profile; if so, close the document and start a new one based on the Web document profile.)

Figure 5.21 Default symbols for Web buttons.

3. This is a nice start, but Illustrator CS4 and CS5 contain many more symbols for button art. From the Symbols panel menu, choose Open Symbol Library > Web Buttons and Bars. You can also click the Symbol Libraries icon (⬚)in the lower-left corner of the Symbols panel to access the list of supplied symbol libraries. The new symbol library is displayed as a floating panel (**Figure 5.22**). The symbols are all very bright and cheerful, but you might want to use a button as a starting point and modify it to suit your design. Fortunately, that's very easy to do. You can either edit the original symbol by double-clicking it in the Symbols panel and entering Symbol Editing mode, or you can just drag an instance of the symbol onto the artboard, double-click the placed symbol, and edit it there.

Figure 5.22 The Web Buttons and Bars symbols include 139 prebuilt pieces of artwork.

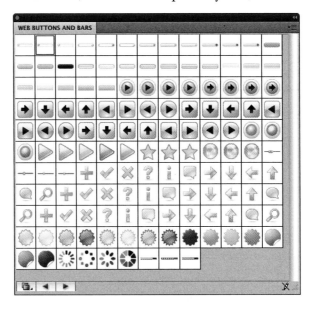

Hover over a symbol, and its name is displayed in a tool tip. Remember that these are just bits of artwork; they have no built-in button functionality. Select the Bullet - Right symbol (➡) and drag it onto the artboard. In the next step, you'll change the color of the artwork.

4. Select the artwork on the artboard (not the symbol in the Symbols panel), and choose Edit > Edit Colors > Recolor Artwork. The Recolor Artwork dialog has two states: Edit and Assign, accessed by two buttons at the top of the dialog (**Figure 5.23**). Click the Edit button to switch to Edit mode.

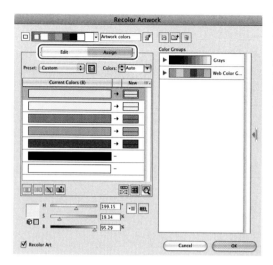

Figure 5.23 The Recolor Artwork dialog allows you to remap artwork colors to another set of colors easily. Access its two modes by clicking the Edit and Assign buttons (circled in red).

5. In the Edit mode, you can move individual color nodes (the small circles) to another part of the color wheel, or you can lock the color nodes together by clicking the Link Harmony Colors icon (⬚) and move the whole shebang, preserving the relationship between the color nodes (**Figure 5.24**). For this button, click the Link Harmony Colors icon, and then swing the assembly of color nodes around the color wheel until you like the change you see in the selected button. Don't click OK yet, though!

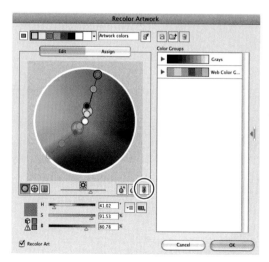

Figure 5.24 To keep color relationships intact but move to another part of the rainbow, lock the color nodes together by clicking the Link Harmony Colors icon (circled). Then rotate the color nodes to another part of the color wheel.

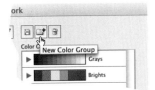

Figure 5.25 Save your new assortment of colors as a color group so you can access them later.

6. You're editing color visually, not picking numeric values. What if you want to achieve the same color shift in another one of the blue buttons? How could you replicate exactly the same swing around the spectrum? You don't have to. Click the New Color Group icon in the upper-right part of the Recolor Artwork dialog to store the new colors in a group of swatches you can access later (**Figure 5.25**).

7. Initially, the new color group is named **Artwork Colors** but you'll probably want to give color groups more descriptive names. Double-click the name of the new color group in the Color Groups column on the right side of the dialog (double-clicking the swatches won't do the trick). The Edit Name dialog comes up. Name the new color group **New Button Colors**, and click OK. Then click the OK button in the Recolor Artwork dialog. You'll receive an alert asking if you want to save changes to the New Button Colors swatch group. Click Yes.

8. Now you can use that saved group of swatches to change the color of another button. Drag the Bullet - Left button symbol (⬅) onto the artboard, select it, and choose Edit > Edit Colors > Recolor Artwork. Alternatively, you can click the Recolor Artwork icon (🎨) in the Control panel at the top of the interface. (Note that it doesn't display in color until you get close to it.)

9. This time, you'll use the Recolor Artwork function in **Assign** mode. Just click the New Button Colors swatch group you created, and the button's existing colors are remapped to the new colors (**Figure 5.26**). Now you're sure that the buttons will match perfectly. Isn't that cool? Click OK when you're done.

Figure 5.26 Assign the New Button Colors group to the left button artwork and click OK.

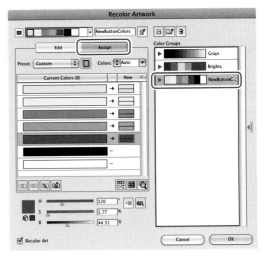

10. Now you'll stack the buttons up so you can control them with InDesign's Object Layer Options. In the Layers panel, double-click Layer 1 and rename it **Back**. Click the New Layer icon (⬜) at the bottom of the Layers panel, and name the new layer **Next**.

11. Select the right-pointing button artwork on the artboard. In the Layers panel, transplant the button artwork to the **Next** layer by dragging the small blue target square up into the **Next** layer (**Figure 5.27**).

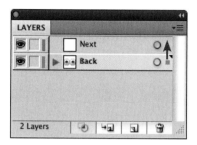

Figure 5.27 Drag the target square from the **Back** layer up into the **Next** layer to move the button to the new layer.

12. Select both buttons and align them vertically and horizontally, using the alignment controls in the Align panel (Window > Align) or in the Control panel (**Figure 5.28**).

Figure 5.28 Align the buttons vertically and horizontally.

13. If it bothers you that those little buttons are surrounded by the oversized artboard, there's an easy way to snug the artboard up to the edge of one of the buttons. Select the button with the Selection tool, and choose Object > Artboards > Fit to Selected Art. If you'd like to stack up a few more buttons in individual layers for practice, please do. Otherwise, save and close the file, and quit Illustrator.

When you use this kind of "button kit" in InDesign, you can choose which layer is displayed in a button state. Why make a single file when you'd use each layer in a separate button? Because it can be really handy when you're making a bunch of buttons to only have to keep track of one art file, and you're guaranteed consistency in size and appearance. When I'm creating buttons for a project, I stack them all up in one Illustrator file, putting each button on its own layer but aligned with all the other buttons, place the file as many times as needed in InDesign, and fix the layer options for each button. Then, if I want to change the color scheme, I fix the one "master" file in Illustrator, update in InDesign, and I'm finished.

Creating Button Art in Photoshop

If you'd prefer to create buttons in Photoshop, you won't have the premade button art that you find in Illustrator, but you can still be very creative by using supplied layer styles and effects. However, you will find one limitation in Photoshop that you don't encounter in Illustrator: While Photoshop opacity attributes are honored by InDesign and Illustrator, blending mode attributes in a Photoshop file are *not* honored by InDesign or Illustrator. For example, a button set to Multiply in Photoshop will not interact with underlying content in Illustrator or InDesign (see **Figure 5.29**).

Figure 5.29 The Multiply blend mode in an Illustrator file (left) is honored by InDesign, but the Multiply blend mode is ignored in a placed Photoshop file (right). Notice, however, that opacity attributes are honored in both formats (the see-through oval area at the bottom of each globe).

Understanding Transparency

What's the difference between opacity and blending modes? It can be confusing, since both concepts are often referred to as "transparency." Maybe this will help:

Figure 5.30 The cyan square is set to 60% opacity, and placed over a solid yellow square. The overlap area is 60% cyan, 40% yellow.

When 60% opacity is applied to an object (whether it's in Illustrator, Photoshop, or InDesign), this allows underlying art to show through at 40% opacity; the total is always 100%. Example: A solid cyan object set to 60% opacity and placed on top of a solid yellow object will produce an overlapping area of 60% cyan and 40% yellow (see **Figure 5.30**). Opacity effects are treated the same in Photoshop, Illustrator, and InDesign.

Blending modes allow objects to interact with underlying objects in a variety of ways: adding the numeric values of applied colors together, subtracting the color values of one object from another, multiplying the values, and so on. The resulting combination may be lighter or darker than the original interacting color, or may be completely different (see **Figure 5.31**). Blending modes are honored *within* a Photoshop file, but lost when the image is placed in Illustrator or InDesign.

Layer Styles

Now you'll experiment with some techniques for creating multilayer buttons in Photoshop, using layer styles.

1. Launch Photoshop CS5 (earlier versions are OK, too), and create a new RGB document, 2 inches wide by 1 inch tall, 300 ppi resolution, with a transparent background (**Figure 5.32**). Name the file **MetalButton.psd** and save it in the **Transparency** folder inside the **Ch_5_Exercises** folder.

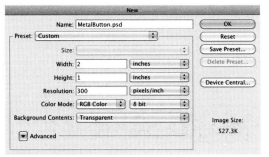

Figure 5.32 Create a new Photoshop document with these settings.

2. Open the Color panel (Window > Color), choose RGB Sliders from the Color Panel menu, and create a color with the values R0-G170-B180 (a tasteful teal). Click OK.

3. In the Options bar at the top of the interface, choose the Shape Layers option (); it's the first icon in the row of options for vector drawing. This allows you to draw color-filled areas with vector edges. While the artwork will render as pixels in Photoshop, having a vector mask makes it easier to modify the shape of the button.

4. Click the Rectangle tool in the Tools panel, hold down the mouse button to reveal the other tools hidden under the Rectangle tool, and select the Rounded Rectangle tool (**Figure 5.33**). In the Options bar, set the Radius value to 60 px, and then click and drag to create a capsule-like button path

Overlap: C100-Y100

Overlap: M100-K100

Figure 5.31 Blending modes: Solid cyan square set to Multiply blend mode (top), and Exclusion blend mode (bottom). Note the color values in the overlapping areas.

Figure 5.33 Choose the Rounded Rectangle tool, hidden under the Rectangle tool, and create a basic button.

in the image. Leave a little room between the button and the edge of the image. Photoshop names the layer **Shape Layer 1**. Double-click the layer name and rename it **Base Button**. Save the file as **MetalButton.psd** in the **Ch_5_Exercises** folder.

5. That's a pretty dull button. You need to give it some depth. It's time to play with some of the Layer Styles that ship with Photoshop. Open the Styles panel (Window > Styles) to view the default layer styles (**Figure 5.34**). In the Layers panel, select the **Shape 1** layer and choose one of the styles. Undo the selection, and then try another style. If you need to undo multiple operations, use Cmd-Opttion-Z (Mac) or Ctrl-Alt-Z (Windows) to step back through time. Undo until you're back to the original dull button, or just select the Effects entry in the Layers panel and drag it to the trash can at the bottom right corner of the panel (it doesn't seem like this will work, until you touch the trash can with the "hand" cursor; then the style is deleted).

Figure 5.34 The default collection of layer styles contains a general assortment of style possibilities, but just a few styles that work for button appearances.

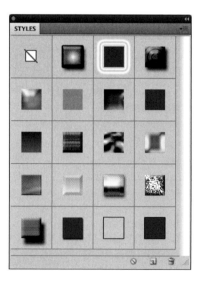

6. The default styles are cute, but there are more styles, and many of them are more suitable for button artwork. From the Styles panel menu, you can select other groups of styles that ship with Photoshop; the Buttons, Glass Buttons, and Web Styles collections are great resources. Choose the Buttons collection, and you'll be asked if you want to replace the current assortment of styles (**Figure 5.35**). If you click the Append button, the new styles are added to the existing assortment. If you click OK, the

existing styles are replaced with the new styles. If you click Cancel, you'll exit the dialog without changing the current contents of the Styles panel. For this exercise, click OK to replace the default set of styles with the Buttons set. (After the exercise, choose Reset Styles from the Styles panel menu to return to the default set of styles.)

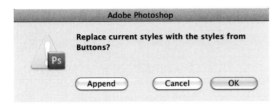

Figure 5.35 You have the choice of replacing existing layer styles, or adding new styles to the panel. For this exercise, click OK to replace styles.

7. If necessary, reselect the **Shape 1** layer in the Layers panel and delete any lingering effects by dragging them to the Layers panel trash. Then, begin experimenting with some of the new styles. You have a lot to play with; there are 32 styles available in the Buttons collection. When you're through playing, apply the Red Star style (**Figure 5.36**).

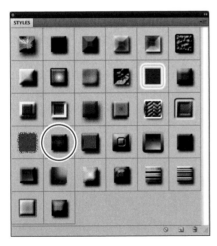

Figure 5.36 The Buttons styles are tailored for decorating buttons. Keep in mind that you can use a style as a starting point and then modify it to suit your tastes. For this exercise, choose the Red Star style.

8. Examine the Layers panel, and you'll see that all the effects that constitute the Red Star style are revealed there. The Gradient Overlay effect provides the star appearance; the Bevel and Emboss effect adds dimension; and the Drop Shadow effect provides the black shadow that lifts the button off the background (**Figure 5.37**). You can easily modify the effects or add new ones to change the look of the button.

Figure 5.37 The Red Star style consists of just three effects: Drop Shadow, Bevel and Emboss, and a Gradient Overlay. That's how easy it is to create your own styles.

9. Double-click the Gradient Overlay entry in the Layers panel to show the settings that were used to create the effect. Experiment with the settings. Choose another gradient from the Gradient pull-down menu, load another set of gradients from within the Layer Style dialog, or try another style of gradient (you can choose from linear, radial, angle, reflected, and diamond). You can also scale the gradient effect. You can even choose another set of gradients to apply (**Figure 5.38**). If you choose another collection of gradients, you'll be asked if you want to append or replace the current gradients. Try the Metals collection, and change the gradient style to Angle. Select the Silver gradient and click OK.

Figure 5.38 To load additional gradients into the Gradient Overlay options, click the little circle-and-triangle icon in the display of current gradients and choose a new collection. For this exercise, choose the Metals collection.

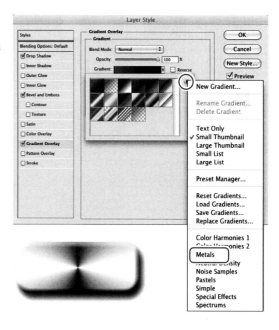

10. To add your new silver angle style to the Styles panel, just hover over an empty spot in the panel. When you see the bucket icon (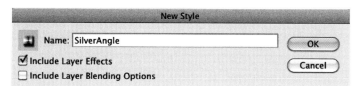), click to add the style. In the small New Style dialog that appears (**Figure 5.39**), name the style **SilverAngle** and click OK. Save the file and keep it open for the next section.

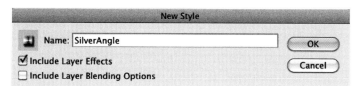

Figure 5.39 Give the new layer style a descriptive name. If the style includes blending modes, check the Include Layer Blending Options box.

Using Layer Comps to Store Image States You've already learned that you can use Object Layer Options in InDesign to control the visibility of layers in placed PSD and AI files, but what if you only have *one* layer with a bunch of layer styles piled into it? You could duplicate layers and apply styles to them separately, but that can add to file size. It would be nice to do it all in one layer. Fortunately, there's a workaround. You can use Photoshop's Layer Comps feature to control the visibility of individual layer styles, and invoke the layer comps in InDesign. Layer comps are a method for storing the visibility, positions, and styles applied to layers. They're a great tool when you're experimenting with an image; you don't have to remember which "eyeballs" to turn on and off to quickly switch between versions of an image. This is particularly helpful when you're showing several options to an impatient client.

There is one caveat: Apply *all* the styles necessary, even though they won't all be visible at once. *Then* create the layer comps to control them.

1. Now you'll build multiple appearances for the button by adding more layer styles. At the bottom of the Layers panel, click the "fx" icon (***fx***) and choose Pattern Overlay. Click the pull-down control next to the blue bubble pattern and you'll find... a grand total of two patterns. But there are more. Click the small triangle-in-a-circle icon on the corner of the two-pattern collection, and you'll find more collections of patterns (**Figure 5.40**). Choose the Patterns collection, and, as you did when you were loading layer styles, click OK to replace the current paltry collection.

Figure 5.40 Choose the Patterns set from the side menu in the Pattern Overlay dialog, and replace the two patterns in the default set.

2. Once the new patterns are loaded, you can hover your cursor over a thumbnail for a few seconds to see the name of the pattern. Choose the Satin pattern and click OK in the Layer Style dialog to add it to your metal button. You can't see the Satin pattern immediately, because it's below the Gradient Overlay effect. Turn off the eyeball visibility control by the Gradient Overlay to see the satin effect, and then turn the Gradient Overlay effect back on. For layer comps to behave correctly in InDesign, you have to create all the effects, and then create the layer comps to control them; otherwise, InDesign seems to get a bit confused.

3. Now you'll add a color effect. At the bottom of the Layers panel, click the "fx" icon and choose Color Overlay. Set the Blend Mode to Multiply, choose a light blue color by clicking the little color block next to the Blend Mode pull-down menu (**Figure 5.41**), and then click OK. Notice that the new effect is automatically placed above the gradient and pattern overlays in the list of effects in the Layers panel. (You can't move effects up and down to change their stacking order, as you can with layers, so this is fortunate; otherwise, the color effect would be hidden.) Save the file and keep it open for the next step.

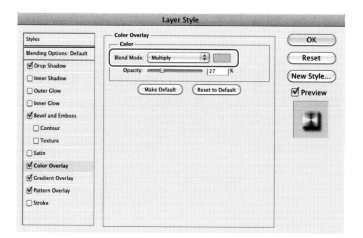

Figure 5.41 When creating the Color Overlay effect, set the Blend Mode to Multiply, and choose a light blue color.

4. Now it's time to create some layer comps. Make sure all the effects are visible (i.e., their eyeballs are "on") before you start. Open the Layer Comps panel (Window > Layer Comps), and turn off the Color Overlay effect by clicking its eyeball; you should just see the SilverAngle gradient applied to the beveled button at this point. Click the Create New Layer Comp icon (🔳) on the bottom of the Layer Comps panel to store the current state of the image. Name the comp **Silver Angle**, and check the Visibility and Appearance options (**Figure 5.42**). Note that you can also store the current position of layers in a layer comp. In this image, you'll be using layer comps to control the visibility of layer styles rather than layers. Click OK and keep the file open.

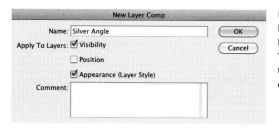

Figure 5.42 Note what a layer comp can store: visibility, layer position, and layer styles. You can even add a comment to remind you what the layer comp is for.

5. Turn off the eyeball by the Gradient Overlay style to reveal the satin Pattern Overlay. Then, create a new layer comp and name it **Satin**.

6. Turn on the eyeball by the Color Overlay style, create a new layer comp, and name it **Blue Satin**. Click the square to the left of each comp and make sure the image appearance changes accordingly. When you're through checking the layer comps, select the first layer comp in the list in

IMPORTANT: The image *must* be saved with the first layer comp selected and active in the Layer Comps panel, even if that comp won't be used for the initial (Normal) state of the button. If any other layer comp is active when the image is saved, it won't behave correctly in InDesign. This is only true for images in which the first layer comp hides some effects (aka layer styles). If the first layer comp involves hiding some layers, all is well. But if the first layer comp involves hiding effects, you must be sure to save the file with the first layer comp active. It's just One Of Those Things. This advice applies whether you're using the image as button artwork, or just as static artwork in the InDesign document.

the Layer Comp panel (**Figure 5.43**), which should be the **Silver Angle** comp. This last step is very important.

Figure 5.43 IMPORTANT: When you save the file, select the first layer comp in the list by clicking the square to the left of the layer comp name, even if that won't be the default appearance for the button.

7. Save the image, and launch InDesign to test the layer comps. Create a new Web document (the dimensions aren't important; this is just a test) and place the **MetalButton.psd** file. Convert the image to a button, and then select the Rollover state in the Buttons panel to activate it. Select the image by clicking the Content Grabber or by switching to the white arrow and clicking inside the button. Choose Object > Object Layer Options, select Satin from the Layer Comp pull-down menu (**Figure 5.44**), and click OK. If the Preview option is checked, you'll see the button appearance change accordingly; it will appear pixelated until you click OK, but don't be alarmed.

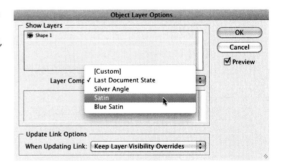

Figure 5.44 Select the image inside the button, choose Object > Object Layer Options, and select the layer comp you want to use for the selected button state.

8. That was fun; let's do it again! Select the Click state in the Buttons panel to make it active, select the image inside the button, choose Object > Object Layer Options, select Blue Satin from the Layer Comp pull-down menu, and click OK. Click the Preview Spread icon (⊡) at the bottom of the Buttons panel and test the button. Save the file if you like, although it isn't used in future exercises.

Layer comps aren't necessary if you're building simple button images with one layer per button state, but they're very useful if the button states will require that you control the visibility of multiple layers. And they're crucial if you're using layer styles on a single layer. Just don't forget to choose the topmost entry in the Layer Comps panel before you save the image in Photoshop.

On Your Own Experiment with duplicating layers, applying different styles or color-adjustment layers, and creating new layer styles. Play with some of the other layer styles available (**Figure 5.45**). There's no excuse for an ugly button!

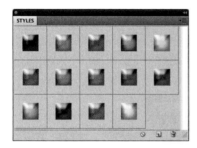

Figure 5.45 Even more layer styles to try on buttons: the Glass Buttons styles (left) and Web styles (right).

Looking Sharp

Although you created a vector mask by creating a Shape layer when you created the metal button, you may be disappointed that the edge of the button is obviously made of pixels when you place it in InDesign. If you create small buttons or buttons with fancy edges, you may lose some definition when you place such images as Photoshop (.psd) files. But there is a way to preserve nice crisp edges, and it's a method that you might want to use for buttons or other Photoshop images with vector content (such as text): Save the file as a Photoshop PDF. The file will still show the edges of vector content as being rendered in pixels when viewed in Photoshop, but InDesign will respect the vector mask and render the edge perfectly (**Figure 5.46**).

Figure 5.46 A vector edge in a placed Photoshop (.psd) file will render as pixels in InDesign (top). But a Photoshop PDF retains the clean vector edge when placed in InDesign (bottom).

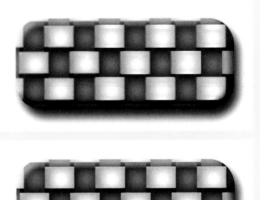

The Photoshop PDF can be reopened in Photoshop with no loss of resolution, by using File > Open. Don't double-click such a file, or it will just open in Acrobat. Think of the image as a Photoshop file in a PDF costume. To other applications it's a PDF, but Photoshop can lift the lid and get to the true image inside.

However, there is a downside to saving as Photoshop PDF. Although layers and layer comps are retained when you reopen the file in Photoshop, they're not recognized by InDesign under Object Layer Options. So use this option only when the rendering of crisp vector content is of most importance. You could still assign separate appearances to button states in InDesign, but you'd have to have a separate graphic for each state if each state will require a Photoshop PDF. (TIP: Create the individual Photoshop PDFs, and then combine them in Acrobat to create a multipage PDF.)

Button Actions

Now that you've explored how to make attractive buttons in Photoshop, Illustrator, and InDesign, you'll explore a few more button actions to add to the actions you learned about in Chapter 2.

1. In the **Novel** folder inside the **Ch_5_Exercises** folder, open the file **Novel_Start.indd**. Choose File > Save As and name the new file **Novel_ Working.indd**. You'll be modifying the navigation buttons in the file to make sure the reader can get to the desired pages. The navigation buttons were created on the master page, so they appear on every page in the document based on the master. This makes it much easier to edit the buttons' appearance or function—you just have to do it once!

2. Open the Preview panel, set it to Preview Document mode, and test the buttons. You'll notice that the Next Page (▶) and Previous Page (◀) buttons work correctly, but the Home button (⬆) doesn't do anything. The First Page button (◀◀) takes the reader to the cover of the novel, and the potential Last Page button has no action and the wrong appearance. But all of these issues are easy to fix. Keep the file open.

In this document, you don't intend to lead readers back to the cover when they click the First Page button; you want to take them back to the first page of the story, which is actually the fourth page of document. But the First Page button action only cares about the first page of the document, regardless of numbering and section starts. So you'll have to use another method to take the readers to the start of the story.

3. All of the buttons are on the A-Master page. In the Pages panel, double-click the A-Master icon to navigate to the master. You'll fix the Last Page button (last button on the right). It isn't a button, and its appearance is incorrect. First, convert it to a button. Select the frame, right-click (Mac: Control-click), and choose Interactive > Convert to Button.

4. In the Buttons panel, name the button **last**, and choose the Go To Last Page action from the Actions pull-down.

5. Now you'll fix the appearance of the button. Select the graphic inside the frame by clicking the viewfinder-like Content Grabber icon (or switching to the white arrow and clicking inside the frame), and then choose Object > Object Layer Options (or right-click/Control-click to choose Object Layer Options). You need to turn off the visibility for all layers except the **last** layer.

You could click all the other eyeball icons to turn off the unwanted layers, but you can accomplish this more efficiently: Just Alt/Option-click the eyeball by the **last** layer, and all other layers are turned off (**Figure 5.47**). This little trick works in Photoshop, InDesign, and Illustrator to quickly hide all but the desired layer. It's nice that it works in the Object Layer Options dialog, too. Click OK.

Figure 5.47 Alt/Option-click the eyeball by the **last page** layer, and all other layers are instantly turned off. Think how much longer your mouse will last.

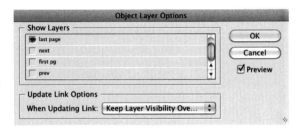

6. The First Page button (⏮) jumps to the cover of the novel. To make it connect to the first page of the story, you'll have to use another method. You'll take advantage of an existing hyperlink as the method for creating a "landing pad." Select the First Page button and, in the Buttons panel, delete the existing action by clicking the minus sign next to the Actions label. Click OK in the alert that appears, asking if you truly want to delete the action.

7. To take the reader to the first page of the story, click the plus sign next to the Actions label, and choose the Go To Destination action (**Figure 5.48**). Notice that the options in the panel change, depending on the action that's selected.

NOTE: Bookmarks, page hyperlinks, and text anchor hyperlinks are all methods of jumping to destinations.

The destinations currently available in the document were created when a Table of Contents was generated for the file. The TOC process automatically generates bookmarks and destinations; that's why you can click a TOC entry in an exported SWF or interactive PDF to jump to the target text. Choose the destination named **I. A New Beginning**, leave other setting at the defaults, and test the button. Save the file and keep it open for the next step.

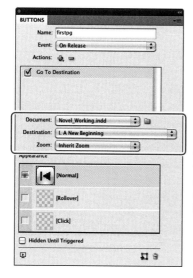

Figure 5.48 The destinations are available because of bookmarks (and their destinations) created during the generation of the Table of Contents. Otherwise, the Destination pull-down would be empty.

8. The Home button should take readers back to the Table of Contents. You'll use a manually created anchor to provide a landing spot for the Home button. Go to page iii of the document (the Table of Contents page), open the Hyperlinks panel (Window > Interactive > Hyperlinks), and choose New Hyperlink Destination from the panel menu. Create a page hyperlink, name it **TOC**, make sure it's targeting page iii, and click OK (**Figure 5.49**).

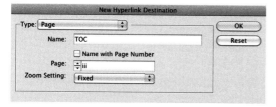

Figure 5.49 A page hyperlink destination works in both SWF and interactive PDF export, whereas a Go To Page action works only in SWF.

You can create three types of hyperlink destinations:

- **Page.** Target any page in the document. While this produces the same result as the Go To Page action, it works in both SWF and PDF export, which might be handy if you're planning to export to both formats. You can choose a zoom option (Inherit Zoom, Actual Size, Fit in Window, Fit Width, or Fit Visible), but the zoom options only work when you export to interactive PDF; they're ignored in SWF export. The hyperlink still takes the reader to the page in a SWF, but does not exercise the zoom.

■ **Text Anchor.** Select text (or just click in text without selecting) to create a target. This works in both PDF and SWF export.

■ **URL.** Store a Web address (e.g., http://www.peachpit.com) or e-mail address (e.g., mailto:you@peachpit.com) to be targeted with the Go To URL button action. URL hyperlink destinations work in both PDF and SWF export.

9. Now you'll hook the Home button up to the hyperlink destination on the TOC page. In the Pages panel, double-click the A-Master icon to return to the master page. Select the Home button (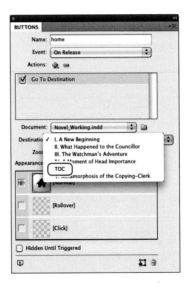), choose the Go To Destination action, and select TOC from the Destination pull-down menu (**Figure 5.50**). Preview the document and test the buttons.

Figure 5.50 Destinations can be created automatically while generating a Table of Contents, or manually by creating a page or text anchor.

10. All the wiring should be working now. You just need to do a little bit of cleanup:

■ On the cover page (the first page of the document), delete all but the Next Page button. Hold down Cmd-Shift (Mac) or Ctrl-Shift (Windows) as you select the buttons to unlock them, since they're locked master page items. Center the Next button horizontally, using Smart Guides (View > Smart Guides to toggle the feature on and off).

■ On the second page of the document (the biography page), delete the First Page and Last Page buttons.

On the TOC page (page iii), delete the First Page and Home buttons. To center the remaining buttons, unlock them all, distribute them evenly, and then select all the buttons and group them; that makes it much easier to trigger the magenta Smart Guide that appears when you hit the center of the page (how did we live without Smart Guides?).

On the last page of the document, delete the Next Page and Last Page buttons, and then group and recenter the remaining buttons. Save the file as **Novel_Final.indd** in the **Novel** folder.

11. Export the novel to SWF (File > Export), select the **SWF** folder inside the **Novel** folder in the **Ch_5_Exercises** folder, and choose Flash Player (SWF) as the format. *Uncheck* the Include Interactive Page Curl option; it would be cute, but redundant since you have the navigation buttons. Leave all the other settings at their defaults.

12. Your default browser should launch after the export is complete. Test the navigation buttons, as well as the hyperlinks in the Table of Contents. Think about the results:

Do you think the buttons are satisfactory?

Would you change anything—color, position, appearance—if it were your own document?

Do you think the buttons are obvious, or do you think there should be a legend page that tells the reader how to navigate through the document?

These are some of the questions you'll have to ask yourself as you start adding navigation controls to your own files. It can be a challenge to anticipate the needs of the audience that will view and interact with your project. Navigation controls should be intuitive, but not interfere with the viewing experience. It's a good idea to enlist other users to test your projects before you deploy them.

A Quick Guide to Button Actions

You've experimented with many of the available button actions in this and previous chapters, but it might be nice to have a list of the possible button actions all in one place. And keep in mind that more than one button action can be assigned to a single trigger such as a mouse click; you can trigger an animation, play a video, activate a sound, and show a hidden button containing artwork, all with a single click. Such sensory overload might be a shock to your viewer, however. Here's a guide to actions that can be triggered by buttons.

SWF and PDF Actions Most actions work in both SWF and PDF export. The actions that function only in SWF, or only in PDF, are separated from the main list for clarity. This first group of actions works in both SWF and PDF export.

- **Go To Destination.** Jumps to a "landing site" such as a page or text anchor. Destinations can be created by choosing New Hyperlink Destination from the Hyperlinks panel. Destinations are also automatically created and named when you generate a Table of Contents. The target of each TOC entry is added to the list of available destinations in the document. Note that destinations do not appear as a list in the Hyperlinks panel; they are only shown in the Go To Destination dialog.

- **Go To First Page.** Jumps to the first page of the document. Note that, to a button action, "first page" is the actual first page of the document, even if it's been designated as "page 35," because you've introduced a section start with the Numbering & Section Options available in the Pages panel menu.

- **Go To Last Page.** No ambiguity to this option; it takes the reader to the last page of the document.

- **Go To Next Page.** Takes the reader to the next consecutive page.

- **Go To Previous Page.** Takes the reader to the previous consecutive page.

- **Go To URL.** Launches the reader's default browser and opens the Web page in the URL link (such as http://www.peachpit.com). Note that the http:// segment of the Web address must be included, or clicking the link will yield an error for the reader. The Go To URL action can also be used to trigger the reader's default e-mail program. To do this, use the mailto format (e.g., mailto:bob@peachpit.com, with no space between the colon and the target e-mail address).

- **Show/Hide Buttons.** This action causes another button (or buttons) to appear or disappear. It's frequently used for rollover effects. The Show/Hide action always requires two players: a button to trigger the action, and another button (or buttons) to play hide-and-seek.

- **Sound.** Triggers a sound that's been placed in the document. Sounds must be in the MP3 format.

- **Video.** Triggers a video that's been placed in the document.

SWF-Only Actions The following actions work only in SWF export, and are ignored in an interactive PDF.

- **Animation.** Plays, pauses, stops, resumes, or even reverses an animation (or multiple animations).

- **Go To Page.** Jumps to a target page. (Note that page numbering is based on the absolute position of the page in the document, not any numbering imposed by the Numbering & Section Options in the Pages panel.)

- **Go To State.** Displays a named state of a multistate object.

- **Go To Next State.** Displays the next consecutive state of a multistate object.

- **Go To Previous State.** Displays the previous consecutive state of a multi-state object.

PDF-Only Actions The last four actions work only when the file is exported to the Interactive PDF format.

- **Go To Next View.** A "view" in Acrobat is a specific zoom factor and page. You can think of Acrobat views as being much like the breadcrumb trail you invoke with the back and forward buttons in a Web browser. What a Go To Next View action accomplishes depends on what pages (and magnifications) the reader has viewed. Go To Next View will only jump to another page or zoom if the reader has already backtracked a bit.

- **Go To Previous View.** Allows the reader to backtrack through a PDF, jumping back to pages (or zoom factors) previously viewed.

- **Open File.** Opens a document file of any format (not limited to PDFs). Note that, for security reasons, Open File will not independently launch an application (e.g., you cannot set it to launch a browser or Microsoft Word). The reader must have the appropriate application to open the target file; for example, if you set a button to open a Microsoft Excel file, but the reader does not have Excel, they will not be able to open the file.

- **View Zoom.** Activates one of the preset zoom factors in Acrobat, including Full Screen, Fit In Window, Fit Width, and so on.

Chapter 6

Exporting and Deployment

You've tweaked and polished your interactive InDesign document, carefully previewed it countless times, and shown it to your best friend over and over. It's time to unleash your project on the world!

As with most endeavors, it pays to start with well-tuned content and follow the rules of the road as you convey your content to the Web. You'll encounter some speed bumps along the way, and a few stop signs. You'll have to yield to software limitations and viewer requirements.

OK. Enough with the highway metaphors. Let's hit the road. (Sorry. Last one. I promise.) Before we examine export and deployment, let's consider the importance of starting with healthy content.

Off to a Good Start

You may be familiar with the technical term *GIGO:* Garbage In, Garbage Out. In print production, high resolution trumps low resolution, CMYK trumps RGB, vector trumps raster. You have to alter your beliefs as you begin creating Web content.

Preparing content for the Web turns some of those fundamentals upside down. In Web reality, low resolution is preferable to high resolution (because of file size), and RGB is better than CMYK. (You don't have to change *all* your beliefs, however; since SWF and FLA formats support vector art, you can still use crisp vector art without having to rasterize vector content.) Some other habits, such as building to correct dimensions and organizing your support files, carry through as you make the move from print to Web.

Document Dimensions

When you begin a new document and choose Web from the Intent pull-down menu (**Figure 6.1**), InDesign displays options for page sizes that correspond to onscreen dimensions. A document based on the Web intent uses pixels as the default unit of measurement, creates swatches as RGB values, and automatically chooses the RGB transparency blend space.

Figure 6.1 Choose the Web intent, and InDesign provides a list of appropriate page dimensions for Web projects.

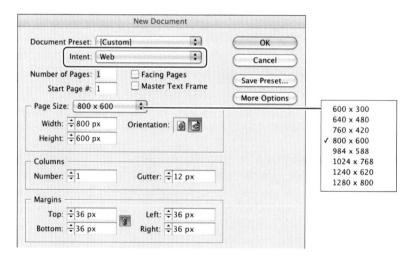

While most users are likely to have monitors capable of at least 1024 by 768 pixels, InDesign's default Web page size is 800 pixels by 600 pixels, which fits comfortably on most laptop screens—even compact netbooks—and provides plenty of room for content. If you're creating a project that you'll present from your own screen, you may want to choose a more generous page size, since you have total control over how the content will be shown or projected.

But what if you're creating a document that will serve as the basis for both printed and onscreen output? You could create two separate documents with common content, but that can be frustrating as you struggle to keep up with two versions of your project, making sure that any modifications are made to both documents. This approach essentially doubles your work—just what you need!

If you're working on a project for which the landscape format is appropriate, build the print version of the document first; this gives you a head start. Then, when you've finalized the content (yes, I realize some clients make changes up to the last millisecond), save the print document, and then choose File > Save As to save a new version of the document. This will become the Web version, but InDesign may be able to reduce the amount of rework you have to do (especially if you've started with a landscape format). Choose Layout > Layout Adjustment, and check the Enable Layout Adjustment option (**Figure 6.2**). Leave the other options at the default settings and click OK. This doesn't change the size of your document. It just gives InDesign permission to massage the content if you do change the dimensions or the margins.

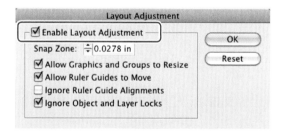

Figure 6.2 The Layout Adjustment feature allows InDesign to massage page content to fit altered margins or page sizes.

Once you've enabled Layout Adjustment, then you can choose File > Document Setup to change the dimensions of the document. While you can't change the intent to Web, you can still choose Web-appropriate dimensions.

Graphics

Think of graphics—whether they are raster images or vector graphics—as the basic building blocks of your projects. Just as you gather up the ingredients before you cook, make sure you're baking with the appropriate graphics.

Color Space

If you're building a project that's solely destined for onscreen viewing, create images and vector graphics in the RGB color space. In Photoshop, choose Image > RGB Color to convert an image to the RGB color space (or assure yourself that it's already an RGB image). In Illustrator, choose File > Document Color Mode > RGB Color. In both applications, you can continue to choose colors from the CMYK color space, but the colors will be rendered as RGB values in the documents set to RGB color space. In Illustrator, spot colors retain their spot color identity, but they will be rendered as RGB when the file is incorporated into an InDesign file set up with the Web intent and exported to SWF, FLA, or interactive PDF.

If you're creating a project that will take both forks in the road (Web and print), start with the print document and create graphics in the correct color modes or print (CMYK, grayscale, and spot), and let InDesign do the heavy lifting for you. If you duplicate a print-destined InDesign document, modify it for Web viewing (see "Document Dimensions," above), and export to SWF or FLA, all CMYK and spot color content is converted to sRGB (a subset of RGB, deemed the "lowest common denominator" for onscreen viewing) during export. This means that you don't have to keep two sets of graphics.

Transparency

If you're converting a print document to a Web document, you must ensure that CMYK content with transparency effects (such as shadows or blend modes) is correctly handled, so you should choose Edit > Transparency Blend Space > Document RGB. This determines the color space that InDesign uses to "do the math" as it exports graphic content and figures out how to render it in final form. You don't have to convert your graphics to RGB; that happens automatically during export to SWF, FLA, or interactive PDF.

When you choose the Web intent while creating a new document, InDesign automatically sets the Transparency Blend Space to RGB.

Be careful when using transparency effects on objects that overlap multimedia content. If the multimedia content is completely covered, you may be unable to click through the stacking order to activate the content, or to use controls (such as player skins in videos). Usually, if some part of the multimedia component is uncovered, it's accessible—and thus, clickable. Always test, test, test everything. And then test again.

Resolution

If you've spent years designing for print, you're accustomed to believing that images should be about 300 ppi (pixels per inch) at final size. Web content, by contrast, is traditionally 72–96 ppi. If you're preparing an InDesign file that will be exported to SWF or FLA, feel free to work with lower-resolution images to start with. But if you're using content that will also be used for print projects, you don't have to perform extra work copying images to make low-resolution versions of them. Just keep the resolution high; InDesign will downsample image content on the way out the door as it exports the project. That's one less thing for you to worry about.

Streamlining Graphic Content

When you add either Photoshop or Illustrator content to an InDesign file, it's best to use File > Place (which should be your habit anyway). But occasionally it's desirable to copy content in Illustrator and paste it into an InDesign file. For example, you might want to change the color of a vector-based icon on each page without having to keep up with several different Illustrator files.

If you paste the content directly into InDesign (rather than placing it), you can manipulate the color and individual paths with InDesign's vector tools. If you attempt to paste an exceedingly complex piece of Illustrator artwork with thousands of points, however, InDesign warns you of the folly of such a move, and takes the law into its own hands (**Figure 6.3**).

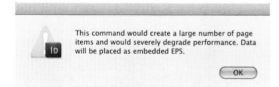

Figure 6.3 Pasting (rather than placing) complex Illustrator files is not a good idea, and InDesign prevents it.

When you export to SWF, all Illustrator content is treated the same, regardless of whether it was placed or pasted. But when you export to FLA, you will find that file size is larger than it would be if content had been placed rather than pasted.

You can economize exported file size by placing graphics (whether they're images or vector art) on a master page if they'll be repeated on multiple document pages, rather than placing the graphics multiple times. If you don't edit the instances of the master object on document pages (for example, by scaling, cropping, or rotating), that object is treated as one object (with multiple references) in the outgoing FLA file. However, if you modify the objects on document pages, they're seen as separate objects in the FLA file, each of which has its own identity.

Exporting to SWF From InDesign

When you choose File > Export and select the Flash Player (SWF) format, you have to make some choices about how the project is treated during export.

General Settings

In the General section of the Export SWF dialog (**Figure 6.4**), you can just accept the defaults and click OK, or you can exercise control over a number of the exported file's attributes.

Figure 6.4 Default options for exporting to SWF from InDesign. Note that the interactive page curl is on by default.

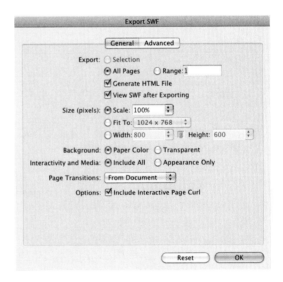

Here's an overview of the General options for SWF export:

- **Export Selection.** You can select an object (or several objects) in a page and export the selection to SWF.

- **Page Range.** The default is All Pages. To specify individual pages, use a hyphen to separate contiguous pages, and commas to indicate discontiguous pages. For example, to export pages 1, 3, and 4, enter **1, 3-4** in the Range field.

Generate HTML File. The HTML file that's generated is a sort of host file, which enables you (or your audience) to view the SWF by opening the HTML file in a Web browser. This is easier than requiring the end user to have a stand-alone SWF viewer, and faster than learning Adobe Dreamweaver to create your own HTML.

View SWF after Exporting. This option automatically launches your default Web browser and displays the SWF file. (This option is not available if you deselect the Generate HTML File option.)

Size. You can specify a scale factor, choose from a list of popular sizes for onscreen viewing (such 1280 x 800 or 1024 x 768), or enter custom dimensions.

Background. Paper Color produces a white background (assuming you haven't covered up the background area with objects or modified the definition of the [Paper] swatch). The Transparent option lets the color of the default browser background show through empty areas, but prevents you from using page transitions or the interactive page curl. You'll have to provide navigation controls, such as buttons, so the viewer can page through a SWF with a transparent background. In the HTML file generated by InDesign as a companion file, the background color is hexadecimal value #999999, a charcoal gray.

Interactivity and Media. Include All does just what you think—it includes all multimedia content and interactive elements such as buttons. If you examine the files and folders created when you export an InDesign file containing multimedia to SWF, you'll see that multimedia files are stored in a separate folder, with **_Resources** in the folder name. The Appearance Only option exports noninteractive placeholders that look like the interactive content but don't do anything. This could be helpful if you want to show a client how the finished piece will appear, without giving away the store by providing them finished, fully functional content.

Page Transitions. Select the From Document option (default) to use whatever transitions were applied to document pages, or disable existing page transitions by selecting None. You can also choose a page transition from the pull-down, such as Box, Comb, Dissolve, or Fade.

Include Interactive Page Curl. The page curl effect is selected by default. While it provides an easy method for viewers to click through a multipage SWF (provided they figure out they should click a corner to turn pages), you'll want to turn it off if you've provided navigational buttons for paging through a document. Otherwise, the page curl will be activated when the user clicks near a corner, and prevent them from using a button that's positioned near the corner.

If you just leave the settings unchanged and click OK, InDesign uses its default approach to image compression and text handling. With the exception of disabling the interactive page curl when it gets in your way, you'll probably get satisfactory results with the default settings.

Advanced Settings

If you want more detailed control over exporting SWF files, click the Advanced button at the top of the Export SWF dialog to explore more options.

Don't be intimidated by the options available in the Advanced mode of the Export SWF dialog (**Figure 6.5**). It offers play-by-play built-in help; hover over the label by any field in the dialog, and the Description field displays information about the option.

Figure 6.5 InDesign provides helpful hints in the Advanced mode of the Export SWF dialog. Hover over a field label, and read the text that appears in the Description field.

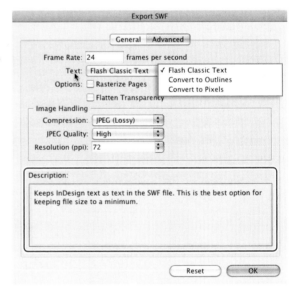

Here's an overview of the Advanced options for SWF export:

- **Frame Rate.** The default 24 frames per second (fps) is the same default setting used by Flash Professional. Higher frame rates equate to smoother animations and larger file sizes. Frame rates above 24 fps are overkill, and values below 20 fps may result in choppy animation.

- **Text.** Flash Classic Text results in smaller file sizes. Converting to outlines results in larger files (because letter-shaped vector objects are seen as objects, not text), and rasterizing text results in the largest file size, because lightweight text content is replaced with pixels.

- **Options.** Rasterize Pages converts all page content (including vector objects and text) to pixels. Flatten Transparency renders transparent objects as opaque objects that retain the appearance of the original effects. Both options disable all interactivity in the SWF.

- **Compression.** The default JPEG (Lossy) option is suitable for most conditions. The PNG (Portable Network Graphics) format supports transparency and 24-bit color, but can result in large files. The Automatic option lets InDesign apply what it considers to be appropriate settings on an image-by-image basis. Unless you have some reason to fiddle with the settings, leave the Compression setting at JPEG.

- **JPEG Quality.** You can select the degree of JPEG compression by choosing a quality setting. Maximum will result in the largest file size (but clearest image content). Minimum will result in svelte SWFs, at the expense of image clarity. The High or Medium setting will usually result in reasonable file sizes without obvious compression artifacts.

- **Resolution.** There's no advantage to choosing a resolution greater than 96 ppi. Perform an experiment using the default 72 ppi setting for one export, and 96 ppi for another. Compare the results onscreen and see if you think the 96 ppi value results in better display quality. As you might expect, higher resolution results in a larger export file size. Unless you plan to place the SWF into a Flash Professional project and use ActionScript to provide a method for zooming in for an enlarged view, there's no need to go beyond 96 ppi, because the viewer won't have any way of zooming.

TIP: If you've been experimenting with export settings and want to return to the default settings, hold down Option (Mac) or Alt (Windows) and the Cancel button in the Export SWF dialog becomes a Reset button. Click that button while holding down the Option/Alt key, and the export settings return to the factory values.

Deploying SWF Files

Once you've chosen the appropriate options and exported your project to SWF, you have to determine how to distribute your project for the viewing pleasure of your audience. Sending your finished piece as an e-mail attachment is usually not a satisfactory approach, unless you have a very small target audience. The sensible solutions are to make your project available on the Internet (or an intranet if it's a production for in-house viewing) or to distribute the project on disc (appropriate for sending out a portfolio or résumé).

Deploying to the Web (or Intranet)

When you export a project containing multimedia components to SWF, the multimedia files are stored in a support folder named after the original file name, plus "_Resources" (**Figure 6.6**). In much the same way as a packaged InDesign file looks next door in its own Links folder to find support art, the SWF file expects the multimedia files to be in the **_Resources** folder.

Figure 6.6 Any multimedia content related to a SWF file is stored in the **_Resources** directory. Don't move, rename, or delete this folder during deployment.

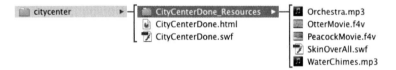

Because the SWF is hard-wired to look for its multimedia support in a particular folder, you must not delete that folder, rename it, or move it. The folder architecture must remain intact for the project to behave correctly.

There is one feature of the final project folder that you *should* change before you upload your project. Unless you want to require your viewers to type the complete directory path of the host HTML file that is generated along with the SWF, you should do the following:

1. Name the enclosing folder something simple, all lowercase. In the example in Figure 6.6, the enclosing folder is named citycenter.

2. Rename the host HTML file either index.html or default.html (I always use index.html). If you do this, the viewer only has to enter your main URL, followed by the name of the folder containing the index.html file. Web browsers "know" to automatically launch an HTML file with that name when it exists in a directory; all you have to do is lead the viewer to the directory, and the browser does the rest. Instead of having to type **www.myparticularwebaddress.com/citycenter/CityCenterDone.html**,

they can just type **www.myparticularwebaddress.com/citycenter**. After you've renamed the HTML file index.html, the directory structure looks like **Figure 6.7**.

Figure 6.7 Rename the HTML file *index.html* to make it a bit simpler for viewers to access your project.

Once you've modified the name of the HTML file, upload the enclosing folder and its contents to your Web site and spread the word.

If you're storing the project on an in-house server for viewing, the process is the same: Fix the HTML name, simplify the name of the enclosing folder, and upload the enclosing folder to the appropriate shared volume on your server. Your IT contact will have to advise you on the syntax you should provide to colleagues who want to access the project (this will vary depending on the network protocol and server type).

Whether you're deploying to a Web hosting server or to the server in your office, viewers will still need the current version of the Flash Player plug-in for their browser. If they attempt to view your project without the appropriate plug-in installed, they'll receive an alert informing them that the content requires the Flash Player plug-in, along with a link so they can download and install the plug-in. If you'd like to provide that information to your viewers so they can prepare to view your project, direct them to the download page on the Adobe Web site: **http://get.adobe.com/flashplayer/**.

CD/DVD Distribution

If you're creating a project that will be distributed on disc, you have several choices for enabling the viewer to experience your project. If you want the viewer to access the project by launching their browser, consider naming the HTML file something inviting, such as **DoubleclickMe.html**. When they double-click the HTML file, their default browser will launch, and the project will load and play.

Viewers can also use Adobe Media Player to view your project without having to launch a browser. Adobe Media Player is available here: http://www.adobe.com/products/mediaplayer.

To allow the viewer to play your project with a stand-alone player (without a browser), provide a link to the download page for the free Flash Player Projector application: http://www.adobe.com/support/flashplayer/downloads.html.

A Projector file is a self-playing file that incorporates all multimedia content; it does not require a separate application or browser to play. When you export to a Projector file, you have options for creating Mac or Windows projectors (or both). Typically, you would create a Projector file for each operating system and include both files on disc.

Note that, even though viewers can launch the SWF file of your project with the Projector application, any multimedia resources must still be available, maintaining the original directory structure expected by the SWF file.

If the recipients of your disc have the Flash Player Projector application installed, they'll be able to double-click the SWF file and launch it directly. Since you can't be assured that they will download the Projector application, however, it's still best to distribute the host HTML file along with the SWF.

Projector files are executables (EXE files on Windows, application files on Macintosh computers). In secure environments, installing any application— even your entertaining project—is discouraged. Additionally, Projector files contain a specific version of Flash Player, which might be out of date.

Instead of exporting to SWF, you could export your InDesign project to the editable FLA format, open the FLA file in Flash Professional, edit it to play as you want (more about that in Chapter 7), and then export the Flash project as a Projector file. If you take this route, it simplifies distribution on disc, since no external program is necessary, but it may require you to do substantial work in Flash Professional to restore functionality that is lost when an interactive InDesign file is exported to FLA. There is no option to directly export a self-playing Projector file from InDesign.

There are still places your project won't be playable. In locked-down corporate environments with security concerns, users might not be allowed to download or install *any* software (including Projector files and the Flash Player plug-in). You have no control over the environments of your viewers, so there's no guarantee that everyone in your target audience will be able to view your project. In anticipation of that, you might consider providing a link to a non-Flash version of your content that they can view in a browser without needing the plug-in.

Wrapping Up

The easiest path out of InDesign is to export to SWF format and count on your viewers to have a Web browser with the current Flash Player plug-in installed. Given that Adobe estimates that 99 percent of computers connected to the Internet have Flash Player (http://www.adobe.com/products/player_census/flashplayer/), you're fairly safe sending your project out into the world with the expectation that almost everyone has the software and hardware necessary to view it.

Note that the 99 percent figure refers to *computers*, and it does not take into consideration that there are popular devices in the marketplace that, while Internet-capable, don't allow Flash content to be played. And that's all I'm going to say about that.

Chapter 7

Exporting to Flash Professional

The theme of this book is "build in InDesign so you don't have to learn Flash," but it can be enlightening to know what your project looks like when it's exported to FLA.

While this chapter is not an in-depth guide to using Adobe Flash Professional, it will introduce you to the general Flash interface and a few Flash functions. Exploring a project in Flash will give you an appreciation for how much work Adobe InDesign CS5 is doing behind the scenes to make it easy for you to create interactive content. When you're ready to dig more deeply into Flash Professional, go to www.peachpit.com and search for *Flash Professional*. You'll find a wealth of resources, from introductory through advanced topics.

Preparing for Flash Professional

If you're working on a project that will require more functionality than you can accomplish in InDesign (such as interactive forms), you'll have to take advantage of InDesign's ability to export to FLA, the native format of Flash Professional. (And, yes, it's pronounced "flah.")

When you use the intuitive interactive tools in InDesign and then export your interactive project directly to SWF format, everything is baked together and you don't have to think about how the complex interactions are accomplished. Nor do you have to edit the SWF file to make it behave. However, any export to FLA format results in substantial alterations to the functionality of interactive content. This translates to quite a bit of rework in Flash Professional to reconstitute lost functionality. First, we'll look at the export settings for the FLA format, and then we'll have a heart-to-heart talk about what falls off during export, and what you can do about that. Finally, we'll do a little exploring in Flash Professional to see what goes on there.

Export Settings

If you want to use Flash Professional to add further functionality, such as behaviors that can only be accomplished with the ActionScript scripting language, choose File > Export and select the Flash CS5 Professional (FLA) format option in the export dialog. The Export Flash dialog appears (**Figure 7.1**).

Figure 7.1 When you export an interactive InDesign project to the FLA format, you can control page range, scale, compression, and text handling.

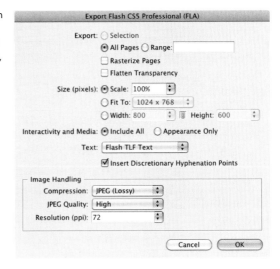

Let's explore the options in the export dialog.

- **Export.** You can choose to export just the objects that are selected when you choose File > Export (handy if you want to test a section of a spread, or if you want to incorporate only a portion of your layout in a Flash animation). Otherwise, select the All Pages option or specify a range of pages. Here you can also choose to rasterize pages or flatten transparency, but all interactivity (such as buttons) will be disabled if you choose either option.

- **Size.** You should build your interactive document to the correct finished size, but this section gives you the opportunity to scale content during export by choosing preset screen-appropriate dimensions from the Fit To pull-down, or by specifying a custom width and height.

- **Interactivity and Media.** If you have multimedia content, choose the Include All option to create a resources folder to hold movies and sounds. This option also ensures that buttons are live and clickable in the FLA file. Any multistate objects are converted to movie clip symbols, and each state of the object appears in a single frame on the Flash timeline. If you choose Appearance Only, no resources folder is created, and buttons retain their appearance but become static objects with no functionality.

- **Text.** The default choice, Flash TLF (Text Layout Framework) Text, is the most flexible option. Text frames that have been threaded together for text flow will maintain their threaded behavior in Flash, and text is completely editable and searchable. For smaller file size, choose Flash Classic Text (which is also editable and searchable). If you've used a decorative font or invoked font features such as swashes, you may wish to choose the Convert to Outlines option. While this limits editability in Flash Professional, it faithfully maintains the appearance of text. Convert to Pixels will also maintain the appearance of text, but will increase file size. Neither outlined nor rasterized text will be searchable.

- **Image Handling.** You'll probably be satisfied with the default option to use high-quality JPEG compression, but your other options include PNG (Portable Network Graphics), which is a lossless format. Understandably, the PNG option can result in larger file sizes (and slower onscreen performance as a result). You can choose the Automatic option, which allows InDesign to determine the outcome. You can also specify image resolution if you want something other than the default 72 ppi. Increasing image resolution will, of course, increase file size.

TIP: To reset the settings in the Export Flash dialog, press the Option (Mac) or Alt (Windows) key; the Cancel button becomes a Reset button. Click the Reset button to start over with the default export settings. Be vigilant. Sometimes the Interactivity and Media setting "sticks" at Appearance Only, so you may have to reselect the Include All radio button.

Export Issues

Because export to FLA format is essentially a translation process, some voodoo is performed behind the scenes to transform InDesign content to something Flash Professional can understand. Because page layout is a very different undertaking from creating Flash content, you can expect some surprises during that translation.

For example, a graphic placed multiple times in an InDesign file will be translated into a single instance of that graphic in Flash Professional, referred to rather than repeated. However, transforming or cropping an instance of a graphic results in a new, separate object in the FLA export.

Effects can add substantially to the complexity of an exported FLA file. For example, adding just the bevel and emboss effect to a circle in InDesign greatly increases the number of items in the library of the exported Flash file (**Figure 7.2**). One solution is to defer the addition of shadows, glows, and bevels, and just add the effects (called *filters* in Flash) in Flash Professional.

Figure 7.2 A simple circle in InDesign (left) translates to a simple entry in the library of an exported FLA file. The addition of a bevel and emboss effect (right) creates a more complex series of entries in the library.

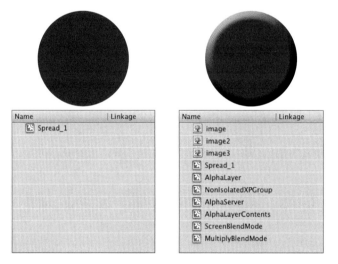

As mentioned in Chapter 6, large numbers of vector objects can slow performance in exported FLA or SWF files. Thus, it's preferable to use File >Place when placing Adobe Illustrator files into an InDesign document, rather than copying and pasting from Illustrator. A *placed* Illustrator file is seen as one object, whereas a *pasted* Illustrator file is seen as all of its individual objects, which increases file size in Flash Professional. However, if you need to manipulate individual components of the Illustrator art in Flash, paste from Illustrator into InDesign so you can use the Modify > Break Apart function in Flash Professional to ungroup and modify complex objects. You can also copy and paste between Illustrator and Flash Professional.

Lost in Translation

If you're creating a project in which you can accomplish everything with InDesign, just export to SWF, upload the appropriate files, and you're done. It's only when you need heavy-duty Flash development that the FLA export is even necessary (or useful).

Here's the bad news: Much of the functionality that InDesign bakes into an exported SWF file is not included when an InDesign project is exported to the FLA format. Consequently, substantial work may be required in Flash Professional to restore such features as multimedia content and animation controls. While this may seem like a bug, consider that the only reason to export to the FLA format is to add functionality in Flash Professional. InDesign feels that "if you're going there anyway, you'll redo all this stuff when you get there." (You won't see that sentence in an alert when you choose the FLA export format.)

Since most functionality is stripped off during FLA export, you might ask why the FLA export option is even provided. Perhaps the most sensible use of the FLA export feature is to bundle up all the graphic content that a Flash developer will require as they build a complex interactive experience to parallel a printed project. If you want control over text placement and layout, InDesign is still a good starting point, since text threading and layout are maintained in FLA export. If you've added interactive functionality in InDesign, export a SWF file for the Flash developer to use as a prototype. It's sort of like sending a PDF to the printer along with your packaged InDesign file, so the printer can use the PDF as a reference for how the finished piece should look.

With the invaluable help of Jean-Claude Tremblay, I've created a list of what's retained (and what's broken or discarded) during export to FLA.

- Hyperlinks and bookmarks are broken. This includes hyperlinks used to take the reader from one page in the document to another.

- Multistate objects are converted to Flash movie clips, and will just cycle endlessly in an exported FLA file, because InDesign doesn't include a "stop" command in the export. And any buttons that were used to control the behavior of the multistate object will have to be re-coded in Flash.

Animations are preserved, but they have no properties or timing controls. They are converted to movie clip symbols, and most coding must be re-done. On the plus side, custom motion presets created in InDesign can be exported as XML files, which can then be imported into Flash Professional. The converse is also true; motion presets from Flash Professional can be saved as XML files and imported for use in InDesign.

Multipage InDesign files will loop rapidly in Flash Professional, like a speed-reading slideshow. You will have to add snippets of ActionScript language to induce stops and starts to make the file behave correctly. Each page becomes a movie clip symbol, and each page generates a separate keyframe.

Page transition effects are lost and must be recreated in Flash Professional.

The ability to click in a page to go to the next or previous page is lost and must be replaced with new code in Flash Professional.

While multimedia content is exported to a resources folder along with the FLA file, the content will not be active in the FLA file. Only the posters for multimedia content are carried through. You'll have to import video and sounds manually into the FLA file in Flash Professional. Consequently, if you're designing a project in InDesign with the intention of enhancing it in Flash Professional, there's no advantage to placing multimedia content in the InDesign document unless you wish to use it to generate a SWF file to show a Flash developer how movies and sounds should be positioned in the FLA file.

Buttons are preserved, but all assigned actions are removed. Buttons are not optimized; even if a button is placed on a master page, each instance in the document will be seen as a separate object, thus increasing file size and the number of Flash library items created. A Flash developer will probably opt to recreate buttons and their functions to streamline the file.

Object names are retained during the export to FLA. Flash developers tend to name objects according to their own conventions, for quick recognition during coding. If you work closely with a developer, ask if you can give the project a head start by naming objects sensibly. Remember that InDesign CS5 gives you the ability to name every object in the Layers panel, and you're also given the option to name animations in the Animation panel.

Editing in Flash Professional

Let's take a quick look around the Flash interface (**Figure 7.3**). It doesn't resemble InDesign, Adobe Photoshop, or Illustrator; its appearance is a vestige of its Macromedia ancestry. While the interface has, to some extent, been "Adobefied," it was important to not disorient longtime Flash users who were accustomed to its original appearance.

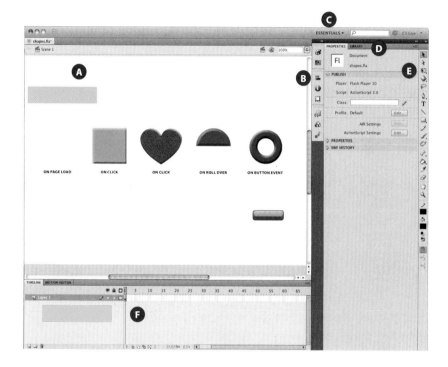

Figure 7.3 The Flash Professional interface. While many tools may look foreign, the conventions you know from other Adobe applications should be familiar.

A. Stage
B. Panels
C. Choose Workspace
D. Properties and Library
E. Tools
F. Timeline

The *stage* is analogous to the page in InDesign. It's where everything happens. You'll see some familiar tool icons, such as selection tools, a Type tool, a Pen tool, and so on. The *Timeline* below the stage controls the duration of animated sequences. The *Properties panel* provides settings for the appearance and behavior of objects on the stage, and the *Library panel* (tucked in behind the Properties panel) lists all the objects in the document.

Keeping in mind that it's not the intention of this chapter to turn you into a Flash developer, you'll now take a look at how a relatively simple InDesign project translates to FLA format. You'll discover that, even though some of the animation behavior from InDesign carries through, it becomes sort of a runaway train. You would have to add behaviors and controls in Flash Professional to replicate what's lost in the translation between the two programs.

First, you'll view a finished SWF file that shows how the project is intended to behave. It may look familiar, since it's based on one of the exercise files from Chapter 4.

1. Launch your Web browser, navigate to the **Ch_7_Exercise** > **Exported_SWF** folder, and double-click **shapes.html** (**Figure 7.4**). Experiment with the behaviors of the shapes. Click the orange square and red heart to trigger their animations. Roll over the blue half-moon to see it rotate, and click the gray button to make the purple doughnut grow. Close the browser after you've experimented with the shapes.

ON PAGE LOAD   ON CLICK   ON CLICK   ON ROLL OVER   ON BUTTON EVENT

Figure 7.4 Play the shapes SWF in a browser (or Flash viewer, if you have one) to see how the animations of the geometric shapes should behave.

2. Next, you'll see how Flash Professional handles a FLA file exported from the same InDesign file that generated the SWF file. Launch Adobe Flash CS5 Professional, choose File > Open, navigate to the **Exported_FLA** folder inside the **Ch_7_Exercise** folder, and open **shapes.fla**. The shapes don't have the gradient fill or the bevel-and-emboss effects that you saw in the exported SWF; this was done to simplify operations and speed up performance a bit. Choose Control > Test Movie > Test to view the running animation. Not only does the activity require no input from you, you'll find that you can't control it at all. No amount of clicking will stop the frenetic motion. You may recall the earlier comment that InDesign does not include a "stop" command; that explains why the animation has run amok. Close the file without saving it.

3. To see what's involved in replicating the behavior of the exported SWF file, you'll open a FLA file that's been extensively edited. In the **Edited_FLA** folder, open **shapes_edited.fla**. Choose Control > Test Movie > Test and notice that now the behaviors are correct. The objects respond to mouse clicks, perform a single animation, and then stop.

4. Choose Window > Actions. In the **Actions** layer, click in the first and only frame (**Figure 7.5**) to view the ActionScript code attached to the frame. This particular bit of code ensures that the orange square will respond to a click in the page.

Figure 7.5 The tiny "a" indicates that there is ActionScript attached to the frame.

5. Rather than be intimidated by the code (**Figure 7.6**), be grateful InDesign makes it so easy to accomplish the same thing without having to write any code at all! Keep in mind, too, that this is only a portion of the code that's required in Flash Professional to make things happen. The more you know about what's required of a Flash developer, the more you will respect all those entertaining Flash animations you encounter on the Web. And try not to feel guilty about how easy InDesign makes this kind of work. Leave the Actions panel open.

```
movieClip_1.addEventListener(MouseEvent.CLICK, fl_MouseClickHandler_5);
function fl_MouseClickHandler_5(event:MouseEvent):void
{
movieClip_1.ID_square.play();
}
```

Figure 7.6 This ActionScript code gives you an idea what's going on under the hood.

6. Choose the Selection tool (⬆), and click the heart. Once the heart is selected, double-click the heart. You should see **Scene 1 > Spread 1** just above the stage (**Figure 7.7**). This indicates that you've drilled down one level into the file content.

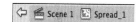

Figure 7.7 Watch the Breadcrumbs bar to keep track of where you are in the hierarchy of the file.

7. Double-click the heart to dig down one more level in the file hierarchy, then click the heart to select it. Below the stage area, click the Motion Editor tab. At the bottom left of the Motion Editor panel, change the Viewable Frames value from **15** to **30** so you can see more frames within the editor. (You can just hold down the mouse button and scrub across the current value to increase it.) Position your cursor over the top edge of the Motion Editor window, and drag upward until you can see more control rows. If necessary, scroll down until you see the Transformation controls. The zigzag line indicates the scale changes that make the heart appear to throb (**Figure 7.8**). Think of it as the EKG of the object as it changes size during its animation. Experiment by dragging on the anchor points, and then preview the animation by pressing the movie test shortcut, Command-Return (Mac) or Ctrl-Enter (Windows).

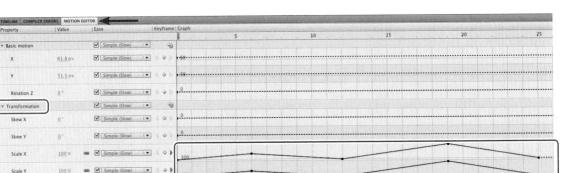

Figure 7.8 The Motion Editor provides an editable graphic representation of the animation applied to an object.

8. Return to the main scene by clicking **Scene 1** above the stage. Double-click to select **Spread 1**, then double-click another object to select it, and experiment with the Motion Editor. When you're finished, close the file without saving it.

Now that you've stuck your toe in the deep and vast pool that is Flash Professional, surely you have an even greater appreciation for the vastly more intuitive tools that InDesign provides for creating interactive content. You should also have deeper appreciation for the Flash developers who make this stuff look easy.

In the next chapter, we'll explore another application that prevents you from having to learn code. Adobe Flash Catalyst allows you to start with Photoshop or Illustrator files and build interactivity with the guidance of something called the Heads Up Display, or HUD.

Don't Be Afraid of Code

Exploring the code-based controls in Flash Professional probably had one of two effects on you: Either you recoiled in horror at what seems to be a foreign language, or your interest was piqued, tempting you to explore more deeply. The exercise wasn't intended to frighten you; it was meant to show you what's going on under the hood so you'd appreciate the hidden strength of InDesign's interactive tools. If you are now curious about what Flash Professional and ActionScript can do, all the better. Maybe you'll be inspired to become a Flash developer yourself.

Chapter 8

Flash Catalyst

Say hello to the new kid on the block. Adobe Flash Catalyst CS5 is available as part of the Adobe Creative Suite Design Premium, Web Premium, Production Premium, and Master Collection, or as a separate purchase. Flash Catalyst enables you to build interactive content and user interfaces from scratch (without coding!), and import artwork components created in Adobe Illustrator, Adobe Fireworks, or Adobe Photoshop.

Or, you can begin an interactive project in Illustrator or Photoshop, creating much of the content and structure by organizing content in layers to give yourself a head start. Then you can import the AI or PSD file into Flash Catalyst and add extensive interactivity with intuitive tools. (Note that, although the majority of this book has been dedicated to the interactive capabilities of InDesign, Flash Catalyst will *not* open or import an InDesign file. However, you can create simple interactive content in InDesign, export it to SWF, and import the SWF into a Flash Catalyst project, as long as the SWF does not rely on external resources such as video or audio files.)

*Three-Letter Acronyms Ahead

While Flash Catalyst enables you to add interactivity with ease, it does have a few limitations. Flash Catalyst cannot animate objects; if you want animation, you'll have to create it elsewhere and import the finished element as a SWF file. You'll find the drawing tools simplistic; there are no Pathfinder operations, and there's no Pen tool. You're limited to drawing rectangles, rounded rectangles, ellipses, triangles, hexagons, octagons, and stars. You can only have one project open at a time in Flash Catalyst; you'll have to close one to work on another. Perhaps you're getting my subliminal message: Build in Photoshop or Illustrator, and embroider in Flash Catalyst.

Flash Catalyst can import AI, PSD, JPEG, PNG, MP3, FLV, F4V, SWF, and FXG (Flash XML Graphics) formats. When you're finished with a Flash Catalyst project, you can publish to SWF, AIR, or FXP (the native format of Flash Catalyst). You're already familiar with SWF; the content can be viewed in a browser or an application such as Adobe Media Player. Adobe AIR is a bit harder to describe. It's a platform for Rich Internet Applications (Get it? *RIA* backwards is *AIR*), which are stand-alone client applications that don't require a browser. The FXP format can be opened in Adobe Flash Builder (a separate application, formerly known as Adobe Flex Builder) for additional development such as connecting with data sources. Note, though, that there is not a pathway to Flash Professional from Flash Catalyst.

There. Now that we've gotten the acronyms out of the way, let's have some fun. You'll experiment briefly with a new document to get a feel for the Flash Catalyst environment, and then you'll import Photoshop and Illustrator files so you can explore the Flash Catalyst tools that allow you to add interactivity to the content.

This chapter is intended to acquaint you with the basics of Flash Catalyst. It's not a full course in doing everything in the application. More than anything, it's meant to convince you that Flash Catalyst puts fairly complex interactivity within reach for users familiar with the way Adobe applications think. If you are reasonably comfortable in Illustrator and Photoshop, you'll soon feel comfortable in Flash Catalyst—especially since the primary function of one of its key features is to hold your hand and lead you in the right direction. It's sort of like a fuzzy puppy. Play with it a little while, and you'll fall in love.

The Flash Catalyst Workspace

When you launch Flash Catalyst, you're greeted by the welcome screen, which serves as a portal to recently opened projects, options for starting new projects from Photoshop and Illustrator files, and online resources such as Adobe TV. The welcome screen also offers you the options to create a new project from an imported Illustrator, Photoshop, or FXG file, or begin a Flash Catalyst project from scratch (Create New Project). Notice that this welcome screen, unlike those in other Adobe applications, offers no option for "do not show again." You'll see this screen every time you launch Flash Catalyst (**Figure 8.1**).

Figure 8.1 The Flash Catalyst welcome screen provides links to recently opened projects, and invites you to import an AI, PSD, or FXG as a starting file—or start from scratch. Take time to explore the resources, including Adobe TV.

The Flash Catalyst environment is only minimally similar to InDesign, Photoshop, or Illustrator. It has a tray of panels on the right side of the screen, timelines and design-time data panels across the bottom, and what looks like a control panel across the top, as well as a horizontal tool panel—but there's where the family resemblance ends (**Figure 8.2**). There are only two workspaces: Design and Code. Don't let the Code workspace scare you; the code displayed in that view is read-only, presented for your edification (or relief—look at how hard you're *not* having to work!). You can't create custom workspaces, but there is a Reset Workspace command for cleaning house.

Figure 8.2 Guide to the Flash Catalyst environment.

A. Pages/States panel
B. Breadcrumbs bar
C. Artboard
D. Heads Up Display (HUD)
E. Tools
F. Panels
G. Timelines and design-time data panels

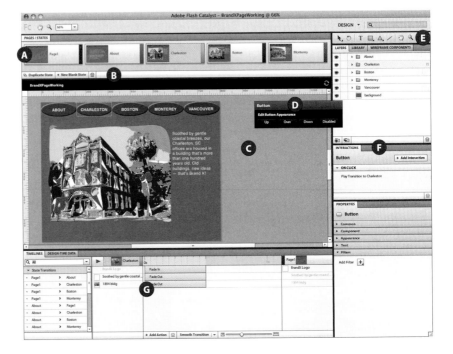

You can't dislodge a panel and use it as a free-floating panel, nor can you completely close a panel. However, you can double-click a panel tab to collapse the panel to a tab-only view, and you can reposition the dividers between interface panels to reveal more rows of the Timelines panel or enlarge the artboard area. As with most Adobe applications, you can press the Tab key to hide everything but the open document and the menu bar across the top. Usually, this happens by accident and frightens the unsuspecting user. Now you've been warned.

In the default Design workspace, the central artboard contains the project. The row of thumbnails above the artboard area contains the pages (also known as states) of the project. These represent the different views that will be presented to users as they navigate to different topics in the exported SWF or AIR file.

You'll use the Heads Up Display (affectionately referred to as "HUD" in the Flash Catalyst interface) and Breadcrumbs bar frequently. The HUD's content is contextual; what you see there depends on what you have selected in the artboard. For example, if you have designated an object to be a button (as seen in **Figure 8.2**), the HUD gives you options for controlling the appearance of the button in each of its states: Up, Over, Down, and Disable. You can position the HUD wherever you like, just by dragging it around by its top edge.

The Breadcrumbs bar (you gotta love that name!) helps you find your way back to the main project when you've burrowed down to modify a single object. If you've encountered Isolation Mode in Illustrator, this will feel familiar.

Basic Flash Catalyst Tools

While you'll frequently do much of your prep work in Illustrator or Photoshop, you can create a project from square one in Flash Catalyst. In the first exercise, you'll create a simple, single-page project to start getting familiar with the Flash Catalyst interface.

1. Launch Flash Catalyst. In the welcome screen, under Create New Project, click Adobe Flash Catalyst Project. Name the project **cabins**, and keep the default dimensions of 800 pixels by 600 pixels (**Figure 8.3**). Click in the block by the Color option, choose the medium dark gray swatch on the first row (#666666), and click OK.

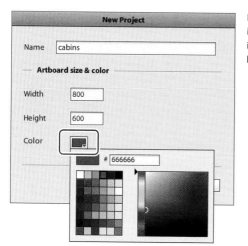

Figure 8.3 You can begin a project in Flash Catalyst and draw and import all content. Choose a size and background color and name the file.

TIP: To get the full-fledged user guide for Flash Catalyst (like the printed copies we used to get in the Olden Days), choose Help > Flash Catalyst Help. Adobe Community Help launches, displaying a list of topics. In the upper right corner of the application, look for the small PDF icon and click on the text "View Help PDF." Once the Help PDF is downloaded (it may take a few moments, depending on your connection speed), it opens inside the Community Help interface. To save the PDF on your computer, click on the small floppy icon (🖫).

TIP: If you'd like to view the completed project in Flash Catalyst before you start, navigate to the **Finished Cabins Project** folder inside the **Ch_8_Exercises** folder, and open **cabins.fxp**.

2. Now you'll import an image of the mountain cabin's front porch. Choose File > Import > Adobe Photoshop File, navigate to the **Ch_8_Exercises** folder, select **RockingChairPorch.psd**, and click Open. Keep the default image import settings (**Figure 8.4**). When you click OK, the image is placed in the page.

Figure 8.4 Photoshop Import Options for placed images. To choose layer comps, click the Advanced button.

Restrictions on Imported Art

- Maximum bitmap image size: 2048 pixels by 2048 pixels
- Maximum total number of pixels: 20 million
- Maximum number of objects: 6500
- Maximum file size: 40MB
- Version: AI and PSD files must be CS4 or later

3. Choose the Select tool (black arrow), hold down the Shift key, and drag a corner of the image to reduce it to about 75% of its original size. Position the image so its left and bottom edges touch the left and bottom edges of the artboard. Nudge the image with the keyboard arrows so it hangs outside the artboard edge very slightly, ensuring that there will be no gap between the image and the edge of the project.

4. Choose the Rectangle tool ( ), and draw a rectangle across the top of the artboard, about 100 pixels tall (you don't have to be exact, because you'll adjust the size and position next). In the Properties panel, set the Stroke to None and the Fill to black (#000000) (**Figure 8.5**). Set the dimensions of the black rectangle to 800 pixels wide and 100 pixels high, and set the X and Y coordinates to 0. While you're there, notice that the Properties panel also provides controls for opacity, rotation, and corner radius. Save the project in the **Ch_8_Exercises** folder as **cabins.fxp** and keep it open.

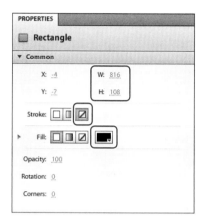

Figure 8.5 The Properties panel allows you to control dimensions, fill, stroke, opacity, and more for a selected object.

5. Choose the Type tool (**T**), and click and drag on top of the black rectangle to create a text frame. In the Properties panel, set the text size to about 50 or 60 pixels, and choose the White swatch (#FFFFFF). Choose the font Arial Bold, type the headline **Mountain Cabins**, and set the text alignment to Center. If the text frame is too small, choose the Select tool and pull on the corners of the frame. Choose Modify > Align > Horizontal Center to center the text frame on the artboard, and then drag the frame to visually center the text vertically in the black rectangle. The project should look something like **Figure 8.6** at this point.

Figure 8.6 The Mountain Cabins project so far.

TIP: To see the tools hidden under the Select, Rectangle, and Triangle tools, just click and hold down your mouse button on top of the visible tool. Release the mouse button once you're over the tool you want. You can also invoke the basic shape-drawing tools with single-letter keyboard shortcuts: M (Rectangle), U (Rounded Rectangle), and L (Ellipse).

6. Now you'll create some button art. Choose the Rounded Rectangle tool, hidden under the Rectangle tool, and click and drag in the gray area on the right side of the project to create a button about 150 pixels wide by 60 pixels high (use the values in the Properties panel as a guide). Fill the button with medium gray (#999999). Note that you can change the radius of the rounded corners by changing the Corners value in the Properties panel. There's no provision for changing the radius for individual corners, however.

7. The Properties panel has three sections: Common, Appearance, and Filters. If necessary, scroll down in the Properties panel to see the Filters section, and click the triangle to the left of the Filters label to see the options. Make sure the button is still selected, click the plus sign next to the Add Filter label, and choose the Bevel option (**Figure 8.7**). Leave the settings at their default values—or experiment, if you like. Save the project and keep it open.

Figure 8.7 Click the Add Filter button to add filters such as Blur, Drop Shadow, Inner Shadow, Bevel Glow, and Inner Glow.

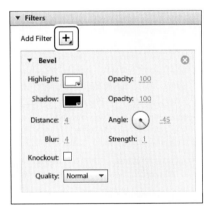

8. The button needs a label. Choose the Type tool, and click and drag to create a text frame on top of the button. Type the word **Photos**, and use the following settings:

   - **Font:** Arial Bold

   - **Size:** 20 pixels

   - **Color:** White (#FFFFFF)

   - **Alignment:** Center

9. Switch to the Select tool, and pull the bottom edge of the text frame up near the baseline of the text. This makes it easier to center the text frame

over the button. Hold down Shift, and click the button object you created earlier to select both the button and the text frame. Choose Modify > Align > Horizontal Center, and then Modify > Align > Vertical Center. The text should now be centered on the button. Keep the button and text frame selected for the next steps.

10. You need two more buttons, so copy the button and text frame to the Clipboard (Mac: Command-C; Windows: Control-C). Paste (Mac: Command-V; Windows: Control-V), but don't re-click; the duplicate button set is pasted into the same coordinates as the originals. Hold down the Shift key to constrain movement, and drag straight down to position the second button. Release the mouse button, then the Shift key. Alternatively, you can just use the down arrow on your keyboard to move the pasted button and its label. Hold down Shift while you press the arrow key, and the selected object moves in bigger jumps.

11. Copy the second button and its text frame to the Clipboard, and paste it into position. Hold down Shift and drag straight down to position the third button. Flash Catalyst doesn't have any "distribute evenly" operations, as in Illustrator. However, you can snap to a grid. Choose View > Grid > Show Grid, and then choose View > Grid > Snap to Grid. Position the buttons so there are two or three grid rows between them, and then toggle off the grid by choosing View > Grid again. Toggle off the Snap to Grid by again choosing View > Grid > Snap to Grid.

TIP: You can customize the grid color and measurements by choosing View > Grid & Guide Settings.

12. Now you'll change the labels on the buttons. Choose the Type tool, and click in the text frame over the second button. (You can also double-click the text frame with the Select tool to switch to the Type tool.) Select the text and replace it with **Rates**. Relabel the third button **Map**. Save the project and keep it open.

13. Now you'll use the HUD (Heads Up Display) to convert one of the buttons to a real, functioning button. Switch to the Select tool, select the top button, and Shift-click to select the **Photos** text. In the HUD, under Convert Artwork to Component, click Choose Component and select Button from the pull-down menu. The HUD immediately changes, giving you options for the button's behavior and appearance.

14. Click the Over state in the HUD, and the display changes. Everything but the button is grayed out, and you can't select other objects. This is so you can concentrate on the button and not change anything else accidentally. Click in the text frame. Then, in the HUD, under Convert to Button Part, click Choose Part and select Label from the pull-down.

TIP: The blue underlined values in Flash Catalyst panels are "scrubbable." Just hold down the mouse button and scrub left and right on the value to decrease or increase it. It's not exact, but it's easier and faster than typing!

15. In the Filters panel, click the plus sign next to the Add button, and add a Glow filter. Set the Glow color to a light blue (we used #96F2FF), and set the Blur value to 10.

16. In the Breadcrumbs bar, click the first part of the breadcrumbs trail: cabins (the name of the project). This takes you back out into the main artboard. Nothing is grayed out now, indicating you're no longer working on a single component. (You can also press the Esc key on the keyboard to return to the main artboard.) Select the **Photos** button, and in the Interactions panel, click the Add Interaction button (**Figure 8.8**). Use the following settings, and then click OK.

⬚ **Event:** On Click

⬚ **Action:** Go To URL (this makes the URL field appear just below the Action pull-down)

⬚ **URL:** http://www.bfparkonline.net (a Web site created for this book)

⬚ **Window:** Open in New Window (this opens a new browser window when the hyperlinked site is displayed)

Figure 8.8 In the Interactions panel, choose the event and action to be applied to a button.

17. Save the file, and then test the project. Choose File > Run Project, or press Command-Return (Mac) or Control-Enter (Windows). The project is rendered to a temporary file, and plays in your default browser. When the project opens in the browser, test the **Photos** button. Roll your cursor over the button to see the glow, and click the button to launch a new browser window and view the target Web site. (If you'd like to set up the remaining two buttons to link to URLs, feel free to experiment.)

18. To export the file, choose File > Publish to SWF/AIR. For the output directory, click the Browse button to navigate to the **Export Cabins Project** folder in the **Ch_8_Exercise**s folder. Leave the export options at the default and click Publish.

19. Go out to your operating system (Mac: Finder; Windows: Windows Explorer), and navigate to the **Export Cabins Project** folder. The export process created a new folder named **cabins**. Inside that folder are two subfolders: **deploy-to-web** and **run-local**. As the names imply, one is for uploading to a website, and the other contains content to be run off a local computer or network volume. In the **run-local** folder, double-click **Main.html** to launch your default browser and view the results.

AIR applications are stand-alone programs that do not require a browser or the Flash Player to be viewed. (The advantage is that no external player is required. The downside is that the AIR application must be installed in order to run. This can be a drawback because some users might be reluctant to install an unknown application, or might work in locked-down environments that do not allow the installation of unauthorized applications.) If you want to export the Mountain Cabins project as an AIR application, follow these steps.

1. Return to Flash Catalyst, choose File > Publish to SWF/AIR. Choose the **Export Cabins Project** folder in the **Ch_8_Exercises** folder (it should still be selected in the Output directory field). Uncheck all options except Build AIR application (**Figure 8.9**), and click Publish. The publish process creates a folder named **AIR** in the **cabins** folder. Inside the **AIR** folder is the finished AIR application, which is named **cabins.air**.

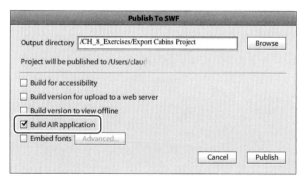

Figure 8.9
If you wish to export to a stand-alone AIR application, choose the Build AIR Application option.

2. If you have no qualms about installing the **cabins.air** application, double-click the file to launch the installer. For security reasons, you're greeted with a warning screen (**Figure 8.10**) asking if you are sure you want to install the application. Since you created the file, it's fine to install it if you have permission to do so on your computer. (You may want to uninstall it after testing it, just to keep your hard drive neat and clean.) The installed application is named **cabins.app**. You can save and close the **cabins.fxp** project by choosing File > Close Project.

Figure 8.10 Because cabins. air is an application, it must be installed. When you attempt to install it, you're asked to approve the installation.

Planning for Flash Catalyst

While Flash Catalyst has some wonderful capabilities, the previous exercise may have also given you some idea of its limitations. Keep in mind that Flash Catalyst isn't intended to be a full-fledged design program. While you can start from scratch, import images, set type, and add interactivity, you will probably find it saner to cook up your projects in Photoshop or Illustrator (assuming you're comfortable in one or both of those applications), as they have much richer tools for creating and editing content. Then you can use Flash Catalyst to put the frosting on the cake.

You should spend some time brainstorming (even if it's just with yourself) at the inception of a project you'll be taking into Flash Catalyst. If you'll be creating multiple pages or states in Flash Catalyst, organize the content in layers in Illustrator, and name the layers accordingly. In Photoshop, organize the content in layer groups that are named to indicate the pages they'll become in Flash Catalyst. This extra preliminary work will pay off. It forces you to think through the project in advance, and it paves the way for easier handling in Flash Catalyst.

Building on Photoshop Files

As you saw in the first exercise, you can import Photoshop files as image content for an existing project. You have options during import that allow you to control which layers are imported, based on a layer comp of the current saved state of the Photoshop file. Effects such as shadows and glows are separated into layers, rather than being treated as an attribute of a main layer (**Figure 8.11**). Effects such as bevel and emboss styles are rendered as finished pixels, and are no longer editable. And since they're "baked in," those effects can't be separated from the object or removed.

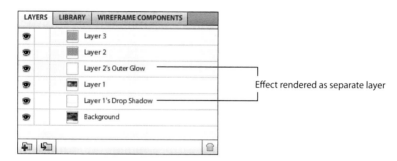

Effect rendered as separate layer

Figure 8.11 Photoshop effects such as shadows and glows become separate layers. Effects such as embossing are baked in, and are not editable (or removable) in Flash Catalyst.

Illustrator has a much closer relationship with Flash Catalyst. Simple effects such as shadows and glows can be controlled in Flash Catalyst even if they were created in Illustrator. More complex effects (such as Illustrator's Punk-and-Bloat distortions or Scribble effects) will be "baked" during import, and cannot be changed or disabled in Flash Catalyst. You'll explore the procedures for importing Illustrator files later in this chapter.

Please don't take these cautions as a criticism of Flash Catalyst. It does a wonderful job of bringing static Illustrator and Photoshop files to life. As you discover its limitations and quirks, you'll find reasonable workarounds and modify your workflow accordingly until you can make it sing.

Now you'll start a new Flash Catalyst project by importing a Photoshop file in which most of the work has already been done. First, you might want to open the image in Photoshop and look at how it's built.

1. Launch Photoshop CS5 and, inside the **Ch_8_Exercises** folder, go into the **Importing Photoshop** folder and open **Brand_X.psd** (**Figure 8.12**). When you import this file into Flash Catalyst, you'll control the visibility of these layers to create five pages—sort of a mini-Web site.

Figure 8.12 In this image, the components for each page were organized in layer groups in Photoshop, to give you a head start when you import the image into Flash Catalyst. The Bevel and Emboss effect that's now a layer style for the button_2 layer will become part of the button pixels upon import to Flash Catalyst, and will no longer be a separate, editable attribute.

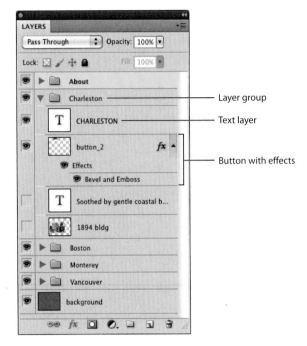

Layer group

Text layer

Button with effects

Each layer group—**About**, **Charleston**, **Boston**, **Monterey**, and **Vancouver**—corresponds to a future Flash Catalyst page. Having the layers organized into layer groups makes it easier to keep straight what should be visible and what should be hidden for each page. The background is common to all pages.

2. Close the image in Photoshop. If you're asked whether you want to save the file, click Don't Save (Mac) or No (Windows). Launch Flash Catalyst, and in the welcome screen, under Create New Project from Design File, click From Adobe Photoshop PSD File. Navigate again to the **Importing Photoshop** folder, and once again choose **Brand_X.psd**.

NOTE: Flash Catalyst assumes that imported images are 72 ppi, so you may be caught off guard by the size of the image when it's imported. What you thought was a 2-inch-by-2-inch image will become an image about 8.3 inches on a side. So build your images at 72 ppi (or resample them down to 72 ppi before importing).

3. In the Photoshop Import Options dialog (**Figure 8.13**), you'll see that Flash Catalyst automatically recognizes the pixel dimensions of the incoming Photoshop file and adjusts the artboard size accordingly. The default settings keep image and text layers editable (rather than flattening them), and crop vector shape layers. Any layers hidden when the document was saved are brought along, unless you uncheck the default Import Non-visible Layers option. To see how you can control the import options for individual layers, click the Advanced button.

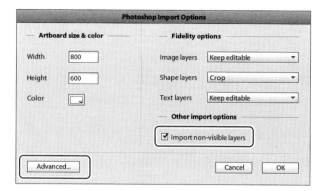

Figure 8.13 In Photoshop Import Options, click the Advanced button to control the import options for each layer. Note the default option to import non-visible layers (usually a good idea!).

Figure 8.13 In Photoshop Import Options, click the Advanced button to control the import options for each layer. Note the default option to import non-visible layers (usually a good idea!).

4. In the Advanced import options screen (**Figure 8.14**), you can choose to import the image as it appeared in a particular layer comp, or in the last document state (the state it was in when saved). You can also specify whether text is treated as editable text, vector outlines, or flattened bitmap content. For this image, just leave all the settings in both import screens at their defaults and click OK. Save the file as **BrandX_Working.fxp** in the **Importing Photoshop** folder, and keep it open.

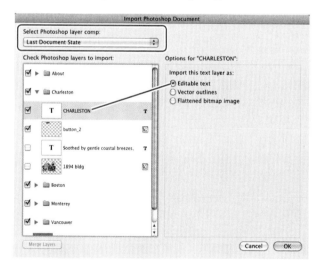

Figure 8.14 In the Advanced import options, you can control the import options for each layer individually.

Pages and States

Notice the Pages/States panel above the artboard area of the Flash Catalyst interface. The terms *page* and *state* can usually be used interchangeably to describe what's seen in a project's artboard area. As the user clicks on a trigger (such as a button), the current contents of the screen are replaced with alternate contents. If the project is a piece with a specific viewing order (such as a story), it makes sense to refer to the alternate content as *pages*. If the alternate content consists of only slight changes to the project (such as a new image in one part of the screen), that would be considered a change in *state*. Both of these results are accomplished by creating a new entity in the Pages/States panel.

NOTE: If you'd like to take a look at the finished Flash Catalyst file, navigate to the **Importing Photoshop > Brand_X_Done** folder inside the **Ch_8_Exercises** folder, and open **Brand_X_Final.fxp**. Close the file without saving (you can only have one project at a time open in Flash Catalyst).

I hope you'll accept the use of both of those terms when referring to the contents of the artboard, and not be confused in this chapter. The nuances of *page* vs. *state* will start to make sense as you manipulate the contents of projects. (When it comes to buttons, however, the term *state* is unambiguous; it refers to the four potential appearances of a button: up, down, over, and disabled.)

In this project, you'll create multiple pages/states from the contents of the Photoshop file. Then you'll convert some components to buttons, assigning actions and multiple appearances to the buttons' states. Finally, you'll tweak the transitions between the pages/states.

First, you'll create the opening page, which will greet viewers when they open the finished project.

1. In the Pages/States panel, double-click the name Page1 to highlight it. Rename it **Home.**

2. In the Layers panel, click the triangle to the left of the About layer group to reveal its contents, and turn off the visibility of the text layer (**BrandXCo is the largest…**), leaving just the oval buttons across the top and the large BrandX logo visible (**Figure 8.15**). This establishes the appearance of the **Home** page.

3. To display some company information, you'll create an "About" page based on the **Home** page. In the Pages/States panel, click the Duplicate State button (**Figure 8.16**). A new page/state is created, named **Page1**. Double-click the name and change it to **About**. In the Layers panel, turn the **BrandXCo is the largest...** text layer (in the **About** layer group) back on.

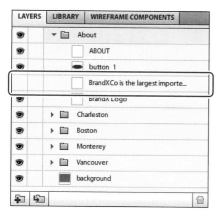

Figure 8.15 Turn off the visibility of the text layer in the About layer group to create the **Home** page.

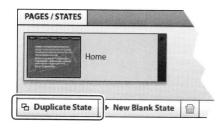

Figure 8.16 To create a new state in the project, you can duplicate the current state, then modify it. You can also create a new blank state.

4. Now you'll create four more pages, which will display information about the far-flung offices of BrandX. For the first location, Charleston, duplicate the **About** page/state, and name the new state **Charleston**.

5. Now you'll change the visibility of several layers to create the Charleston page. If necessary, click on the Charleston page thumbnail in the Pages/States panel to make it active. In the **About** layer group, turn off the eyeball visibility control by the text layer (**BrandXCo is the largest...**) to hide it, then hide the **BrandX Logo** layer. Click the triangle to the left of the **Charleston** layer group to show its contents. Turn on the visibility of the text layer (**Soothed by...**) and the **1894 bldg** layer (**Figure 8.17**).

Figure 8.17 Creating the **Charleston** page/state. Turn off the text and logo layers in the **About** layer group, and turn on the hidden layers on the **Charleston** layer group.

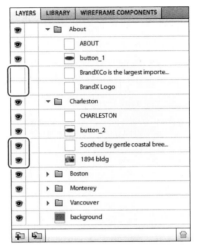

This is the pattern that you'll follow for the remaining pages. You'll leave the oval button layers and their related type layers visible for all versions, and you'll turn on the text and graphic for each location, while hiding the text and graphic for each of the other versions.

6. Duplicate the **Charleston** page/state, and name the new state **Boston**. For the **Boston** state, turn off the **Charleston** text layer (Soothed by gentle...) and graphic layer, **1894 bldg**. In the **Boston** layer group, turn on the **Trinity Church** graphic layer and the **Our Boston offices...** text layer (**Figure 8.18**).

Figure 8.18 Layer settings for the **Boston** layer (are you starting to sense a trend?).

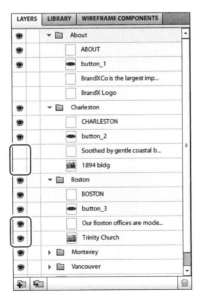

7. Following the same pattern, create two more pages, for Monterey and Vancouver. Turn off the layers containing the descriptive text and the graphics for the other locations, and reveal the text and graphics layers appropriate for the **Monterey** and **Vancouver** layers. Leave the oval buttons and their text (**ABOUT, CHARLESTON, BOSTON,** etc.) visible in all pages/states (**Figure 8.19**). Save the file and keep it open.

Figure 8.19 Using the other location pages as a guide, create the Monterey (left) and Vancouver (right) pages.

Navigation Buttons

The viewers of the final project will use the large oval buttons at the top of the artboard to navigate to the information about BrandX locations.

1. Select the text frame containing the text **ABOUT** and Shift-click to select the oval button behind the text. The Heads Up Display (HUD) wakes up, giving you the option to Convert Artwork to Component (**Figure 8.20**).

Figure 8.20 When you select an object in the artboard, the HUD displays available options. Click Choose Component to convert the oval and text into a button.

2. In the HUD, click Choose Component, and select the Button option from the pull-down list that appears. (For all available component types, see the sidebar, "Component Types.")

Immediately, the HUD changes to show you the button appearance options (**Figure 8.21**).

Figure 8.21 The HUD allows you to specify a different appearance for each of the four button states.

3. In the Interactions panel, click the Add Interaction button (**Figure 8.22**). Leave the trigger at the default (On Click), and the action at the default (Play Transition to State). Click the Choose State pull-down, choose the **About** page/state you created earlier, and click OK.

Figure 8.22 In the Interactions panel, click Add Interaction to reveal the options. For the **About** button, choose Play Transition to State.

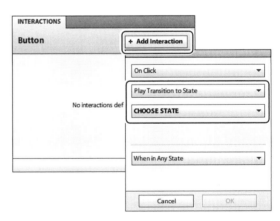

4. Now you'll add a glow to the Over state of the **About** button. In the HUD display, click the Over option. Select the **About** button (the ellipse, not the text). In the Filters section of the Properties panel, click the plus sign

to the right of the Add Filter option and choose the Glow option (**Figure 8.23**). If you don't see the Filters section of the Properties panel, you may have to click the triangles to the left of the Common, Component, Appearance, and Text sections to collapse their contents in order to make room for the Filters section, which is at the very bottom of the Properties panel. Click the blue block labeled Color, and choose the white swatch (#FFFFFF).

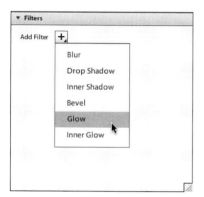
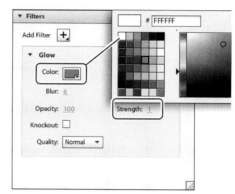

Figure 8.23 Choose the Glow filter, and then click the color block (initially blue) to choose a color for the glow. For the **About** button, add a white (#FFFFFF) glow.

Why Does #FFFFFF = White?

In the language of HTML (Hypertext Markup Language), colors are described using a hexadecimal system (base 16). Don't worry; you don't have to think in hex. You can pick colors from several color systems in Flash Catalyst, including the Color Picker (the round "spectrum" source), but they'll be expressed in the Flash Catalyst file by hexadecimal code. Hex codes for colors consist of a pound sign (#) plus six numbers. The six numbers are actually three pairs of numbers, describing Red, Green, and Blue values. A full explanation of the hex color system is beyond the scope of this chapter, but if you're curious about hexadecimal numbers and how they relate to color on the Web, check out this online resource: http://www.w3schools.com/Html/html_colors.asp.

5. Click the blue number by the Strength setting, and change it to **2** to make the white glow more pronounced. (You can also "scrub" the number by holding down the mouse button and moving left and right. While this is an easy way to quickly decrease or increase the value, it's hard to enter an exact value with the scrubbing method.)

6. Working on the **About** button attributes has taken you into component editing mode. To return to the main work area, click the project name in the Breadcrumbs bar (**Figure 8.24**). Save the file and keep it open.

Figure 8.24 Click the project name in the Breadcrumbs bar to return to the main artboard window.

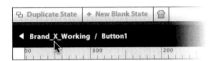

7. Test the **About** button to see if its appearance and behavior are correct. Choose File > Run Project, and Flash Catalyst generates temporary files to display in your default Web browser. In the browser, roll your mouse over the **About** button. Does it glow? Click the **About** button to jump to the **About** page/state. Close the browser window. If you want to test your project frequently as you work (which is a good idea), leave the browser running in the background.

8. Return to Flash Catalyst so you can set up the remaining buttons. The steps for the other buttons follow the same pattern as those you followed when creating the **About** button:

    a. Select the location text (the city name) and the oval button behind it.

    b. In the HUD, choose Convert Artwork to Component and select Button for the component type.

    c. In the Interactions panel, click Add Interaction and choose the Play Transition to State option, choosing the appropriate target state (e.g., choose the **Charleston** state as the target for the **Charleston** button).

    d. In the HUD, select the Over option, select the button, and use the settings in the Filter panel to apply a Glow filter. As with the **About** button, select white (#FFFFFF) for the color, and set the Strength to 2.

    e. Use the Breadcrumbs bar to return to the main project window and start on the next button.

    f. Return to the main project window after you've finished the last button, and test the project. Use the shortcut for Run Project: Press Command-Return (Mac) or Control-Enter (Windows). Return to Flash Catalyst, save the project, and keep it open.

You'll soon find yourself falling into a rhythm. While the button-making procedure is a bit tedious, it's not truly complicated. Once you've created the second button, you'll find that it's faster to create each successive button. And the repetition is a great way to remember the steps.

Flash Catalyst Drawing Tools

You're missing one navigational aid. There's no way for the viewer to get back to the Home screen unless they refresh the browser. You'll use Flash Catalyst drawing and text tools to create a button that takes the viewer back to the Home screen.

1. In the Layers panel, click the Create New Layer icon at the lower left of the panel and create a new layer. The new layer, named **Layer 1**, should appear at the top of the list in the Layers panel. If not, you can select the layer and move it to the correct position by dragging in the Layers panel, just as you would in Photoshop, Illustrator, or InDesign. Double-click the name of the new layer to name it **Home Button** (**Figure 8.25**).

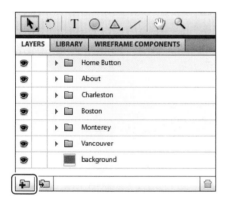

Figure 8.25 Click the Create New Layer icon to create a new layer. Name it **Home Button**. This is where you'll create a common button that will appear in all pages/states.

2. In the Pages/States panel, click the **About** page/state. (It actually doesn't matter which state you choose, but this will let you work methodically from left to right as you add the new button to every page/state. It also ensures that the button won't cover up any of the text on the About page.) You'll draw an ellipse in the lower-right area of the artboard that will be the basis of a button that appears in all pages/states to lead the viewer back to the initial **Home** page. In the Tools panel (above the Layers panel), click the Rectangle/Ellipse icon to reveal the Rectangle, Rounded Rectangle, and Ellipse drawing tools (**Figure 8.26**). Choose the Ellipse

tool and draw an ellipse in the lower-right corner of the artboard. Make it about 75% of the width of the large oval (aka elliptical) buttons at the top of the project.

Figure 8.26 To draw a circle or ellipse, choose from the Rectangle/Ellipse pull-down in the Tools panel.

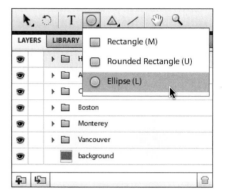

3. The Properties panel contains three sections: Common, Appearance, and Filters. In the Common section (**Figure 8.27**), set the Stroke attribute of the new ellipse to None (☑), and the Fill attribute to a light gray (we used #999999 just because it's such a cool hex number). Keep the ellipse selected.

Figure 8.27 Choose the Stroke and Fill attributes in the Common Properties panel.

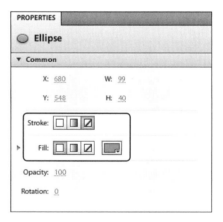

4. In the Filters section, choose Bevel from the Add Filter pull-down and set the Distance value to 2.

5. Choose the Text tool, and click and drag to create a text frame on the ellipse. This will hold the button label. Click inside the text frame and type **Home**, and then select the text to change its formatting. In the Common subpanel, choose the following settings:

   - **Font:** Arial Bold

   - **Size:** 16 (adjust as necessary to fit inside your ellipse)

   - **Color:** Light Gray (#CCCCCC, another amusing hex value)

   - **Alignment:** Center

6. Using the Select tool ( ), pull on the corners of the text frame so it's close to the type (without causing overset text). Then, Shift-click to select the ellipse, and choose Modify > Align > Horizontal Center. Since there's no way to vertically center text in a frame (as you can in InDesign), you'll have to—gasp!—eyeball it (**Figure 8.28**). Deselect the ellipse by Shift-clicking in it again, leaving just the text frame selected. Using the arrow keys on your keyboard, nudge the **Home** text frame into position. Save the project and keep it open.

Figure 8.28 Center the **Home** text vertically and horizontally in the ellipse.

7. Select both the ellipse and the **Home** text and, in the HUD, convert the artwork to a button. Using the Interactions panel, add an interaction that sends viewers back to the **Home** page/state: Click Add Interaction and choose the Play Transition to State option. Choose the **Home** page/state as the target and click OK.

8. Rather than adding a Glow effect to the entire button for the Over state, you'll just have the text glow. It's a subtle effect, but it still provides visual feedback to the viewer that something is happening. Visual feedback keeps the viewer engaged and lets them know they're on the right track. It's a little extra work, but it does add to the viewing experience. In the HUD, select the Over state, which puts you in component editing mode. Select just the text frame (not the ellipse) and, in the Filters panel, choose the Glow option and use the following settings:

   - **Color:** Black (#000000)

   - **Blur:** 20

   - **Opacity:** 100

   - **Strength:** 1

9. Return to the main project window by using the Breadcrumbs bar. Now you'll make the **Home** button visible on the location pages, starting with the Charleston location. Select the **Charleston** page/state in the Pages/States panel, and turn on the visibility of the **Home** button (**Figure 8.29**). You'll have to click the triangle next to the **Home** Button layer to display and select the button object; just setting the layer visibility isn't sufficient.

Figure 8.29 Make the **Home** button visible in all location states.

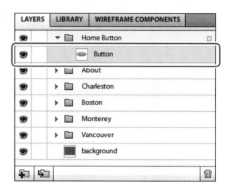

TIP: A faster way to add an object to all states is by right-clicking in the object and selecting Share To State > All States. You can also target individual pages/states with this method.

The **Home** button also needs to appear on the **Boston**, **Monterey**, and **Vancouver** pages/states. Select the button on the **Charleston** page/state, right-click (Mac: Control-click), and choose Share To State > All States. Since you don't need the **Home** button on the **Home** page/state, select the **Home** page/state and turn off the visibility of the **Home** button in the Layers panel (or just delete the button from the **Home** page/state; it accomplishes the same thing). When you're finished, test the project by pressing Command-Return (Mac) or Control-Enter (Windows) so you can preview the project. Make sure the **Home** button appears on the correct pages/states and takes you back to the **Home** page/state. Test the glow effect when you roll over the button. Save the project and keep it open.

Transitions

By default, changing pages/states just replaces the current contents of the screen with the alternate contents. If you'd like a more graceful transition (or even a fancy 3D rotation), use the controls in the Timelines panel (**Figure 8.30**).

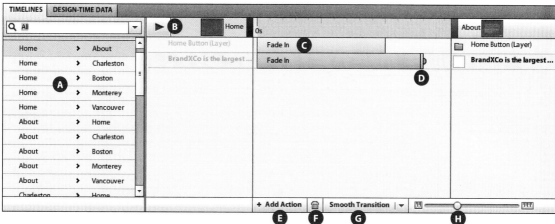

Figure 8.30 Controlling transitions in the Timelines panel.

A. State Transitions list
B. Play transition
C. Effects bar
D. Resize handle to change duration
E. Add action
F. Delete transition
G. Add smooth transition (default)
H. Change scale of timeline increments (for fine tuning)

1. First, you'll create a smooth fading transition between the initial **Home** state and the **About** state. In the Pages/States panel, select **Home** Home page/state. In the State Transitions area of the Timelines panel, select the first transition, Home > About. Click the Smooth Transition bar at the bottom of the timeline ("G" in **Figure 8.30**) to apply the default 0.5-second transition. Click the Play button (▶) at the top of the Timelines panel to view the results.

2. Now you'll modify the fade-in of the **About** state so the button appears first, and the text fades in more slowly. The bars representing the length of transitions can be modified by dragging the small handle on the right end of the bar; you can also reposition the bars by dragging them in the timeline. Repositioning a transition bar changes the time at which a transition begins, not its duration. Select the transition bar for the **About** text (**BrandX is the largest...**), and then drag the small handle to the right until it reaches the 1 second mark, represented on the time ruler as **1s** **Play** the transition to view the results. If you're satisfied with the results, save the file. Feel free to experiment with the transition sliders.

3. To set the transition between the **Home** state and the **Charleston** state, select the Home > Charleston transition in the list of transitions. Click the Smooth Transition bar at the bottom of the timeline to add the default half-second transition. Drag the handle on the right end of the slider for the graphic (**1894 bldg**) to extend the time to the 1 second mark, and preview the results. Save the file and keep it open.

Figure 8.31 You can alter the default Smooth Transition Options to affect future (and existing) transitions.

Figure 8.32 Changing the Smooth Transition settings affects all transitions that use the default Smooth Transition.

TIP: Notice that small thumbnails above the timeline show the starting and ending state. They can help keep you oriented as you wade through multiple transitions. You're also probably starting to see the wisdom of naming your pages/states sensibly, to make it easier to keep track of what you're doing. Trying to remember what "Page1," "Page2," or "Page3" represents can make your work harder.

4. You can modify the default settings for smooth transitions and speed up your work. Click the small downward-pointing triangle to the right of the Smooth Transition bar to display the Smooth Transition Options panel (**Figure 8.31**). For example, if you'd like all transitions to be 1.5 seconds long, change the Duration setting to 1.5. Then you can quickly add a 1.5-second transition by simply clicking the Smooth Transition bar, without having to drag any slider controls.

5. For this project, change the Duration in the Smooth Transition Options panel to 1.5 seconds, choose the Smart Smoothing option, and check the Overwrite Existing Effects option. Click OK, and then observe how the transition sliders have changed (**Figure 8.32**).

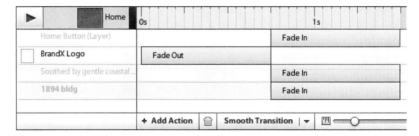

The options in the Smooth Transition Options panel are as follows:

- **Duration:** The total time of the transition from start to end.

- **Timing—Simultaneous:** Each transition effect starts and stops simultaneously.

- **Timing—Smart Smoothing:** Creates a staggered set of transitions. After objects fade out, all resize and move effects play, followed by objects fading in.

- **Overwrite Existing Effects:** Changing values in this dialog will affect previous transitions that use the default transition. Leave this unchecked to affect only future transitions.

6. This project has 30 transitions. The project consists of six pages/states, and each page/state could potentially transition to five other states. If you had to modify each transition individually, the fun would soon wear off. This is why changing the Smooth Transition settings is beneficial. In the State Transitions list, select the Home > Charleston transition, then scroll down and Shift-click the last transition, Vancouver > Monterey. Click the Smooth Transition bar, and all of the selected transitions take on the

new settings. Very easy! Test the project transitions by choosing File > Run Project or by using the keyboard shortcuts, Command-Return (Mac) or Control-Enter (Windows).

7. If you decide that the 1.5-second transition is too slow for your tastes, change the Smooth Transition settings, checking the Overwrite Existing Effects option, and test the project again.

8. If you'd like to export the project to run locally, or want to upload the final exported files to a Web server for testing, choose File > Publish to SWF/AIR. In the export dialog, browse to the **Importing Photoshop** folder (or another location of your choice), accept the default settings, and click OK. Flash Catalyst will export two versions: one for local viewing, and one for posting on a remote server.

When you publish to SWF with the default settings, Flash Catalyst creates a folder named after the project, and generates a "host" HTML file inside that folder named **Main.html**. Some Web servers don't automatically launch a file with that name, so the user must type it. If you rename that HTML file either **index.html** or **default.html**, the user can just navigate to the parent directory of the file, rather than having to type the complete directory path, and the server will automatically launch the appropriately named file. You may want to simplify the name of the containing folder, too. You can see which URL would be easier for your audience to type:

- www.mybrandxsite.com/deploy-to-web/Main.html

- www.mybrandxsite.com/info

9. Change the name of the **deploy-to-web** folder to **info**. Then change the name of **Main.html** to **index.html**. If you upload the **info** folder to your Web server, the viewer will only have to type the URL for your Web site, followed by /**info**. Less typing, more enjoyable viewing. Save the project and close the file.

Now that you've completed the project, consider how the layer organization in Photoshop gave you a head start for the Flash Catalyst project. Sensible layer group naming and consistent arrangement of layers within the layer groups made the project much easier to handle in Flash Catalyst. And working methodically in Flash Catalyst should have made it easier for you to see patterns in the procedures you had to perform, such as creating pages/states and setting up buttons for navigation. Remember this when you start creating your own projects from scratch. Make it easy on yourself.

TIP: Did you notice that the **Home** button doesn't seem to fade in or out? That's because it appears on five of the six pages/states. Since its situation doesn't change from page to page, there's no need for a transition. If you click the **Home** button while you're previewing the project in a browser, you'll see that it fades out during the transition to the **Home** page because it doesn't exist on that page/state.

Building on Illustrator Files

You'll find that starting a Flash Catalyst project based on an Illustrator file is a bit easier than working with Photoshop files. As mentioned earlier, Illustrator content is more faithfully translated when imported into Flash Catalyst, giving you a bit more flexibility.

You can pave the way from Illustrator into Flash Catalyst, making the transition even smoother. A few tips:

- Choose the Flash Catalyst document profile in Illustrator when you start building the document, and the correct settings are automatically chosen for color mode, ppi, document dimensions, and pixel grid.

- Ensure that images are 72 ppi.

- Images should be in RGB color mode.

- Embed images or ensure that they are correctly linked (image content becomes embedded in the Flash Catalyst document anyway).

- Any symbols in imported Illustrator files become optimized graphics in Flash Catalyst, and appear in the Library panel. If a symbol is used several times in an Illustrator file, you can reduce the size of the Flash Catalyst file by having just one copy of the optimized graphic and sharing that object among multiple pages/states. You can edit a single instance in Flash Catalyst by selecting it and choosing Modify > Break Apart Graphic.

- Use Align to Pixel Grid when creating vector components in Illustrator (**Figure 8.33**). This is especially beneficial for vertical and horizontal objects, keeping them crisp, with no anti-aliasing to soften edges. (The setting has no effect on text.)

Figure 8.33 Select objects in Illustrator and choose the Align to Pixel Grid option in the Transform panel. If you build the file on the Flash Catalyst document profile, this is checked automatically.

Building the Project

In this exercise, you'll create a tourism promotional piece for the state of Vermont, using an Illustrator file as the starting point.

1. First you'll examine an Illustrator file to see how it's built. Launch Illustrator, navigate to the **Importing Illustrator** folder inside the **Ch_8_Exercises** folder, and open **VermontStart.ai**. If you don't have Illustrator, you can get an idea how the file is set up in **Figure 8.34**. Several layers are currently locked to protect their content until you begin to modify components in Flash Catalyst. After you've poked around a little bit, close the file without saving.

Figure 8.34 The Vermont project organized in Illustrator.

2. Launch Flash Catalyst and, in the welcome screen, under Create New Project from Design File, choose From Adobe Illustrator File. Navigate to the **Importing Illustrator** folder and select **VermontStart.ai**. If you receive an alert about hyphenation settings, ignore it and click OK to dismiss the alert. Save the project as **VermontWorking.fxp** in the **Importing Illustrator** folder.

Creating a Scroll Panel You'll create a panel containing scrolling text and a vertical scroll bar to control the text.

1. In the Layers panel, unlock the **Text field and controls** layer by clicking on the padlock next to the layer name. Select the Zoom tool (🔍), and zoom in on the text at the bottom of the artboard (**Vermont's beautiful landscapes...**). You can also use the keyboard shortcuts you know so

well from other Adobe applications: Command-spacebar-click (Mac) or Control-spacebar-click (Windows).

2. Choose the Text tool and click in the text frame containing the white text. Still using the Text tool, click the small square containing a blue triangle on the bottom edge of the text frame (**Figure 8.35**). The frame will expand, revealing all the overset text. This just makes the overset text available in Flash Catalyst; the original dimensions of the frame will be used as the basic scroll panel, and the text will scroll within the area.

Figure 8.35 Click the overset indicator (circled) to expand the text frame.

Vermont's beautiful landscapes are compelling all year around. From the snowy mountainsides during Winter to the rich greenery of maple-syrup time in Spring, you'll feel as if you're living in a greeting card! Summer's gentle temperatures are

3. Now you'll create the vertical scroll bar that will control the text, and establish a relationship between the scroll bar and the text so it can make the text scroll up and down. Choose the Select tool and click on the tall, narrow black rectangle to the right of the text. Hold down the Shift key and click the small green rectangle so both objects are selected. The HUD wakes up and offers to help. Choose Vertical Scrollbar from the list of options (**Figure 8.36**).

Figure 8.36 Under Choose Component, select Vertical Scrollbar to designate the two rectangles as a scrolling control for the text.

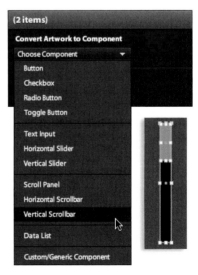

4. The HUD prompts you to designate the individual parts of the scroll bar by displaying a hint, telling you to select and assign the parts of the scroll bar so it will work (**Figure 8.37**). The green rectangle will be the Thumb (the part that moves up and down), and the black rectangle will be the Track.

Figure 8.37 The HUD tells you to select the parts of the vertical scroll bar and assign their function.

5. Select the black rectangle, click Choose Part in the HUD, and select Track (Required) from the list of parts. Then, select the green rectangle and designate it as Thumb (Required). As you can see, the HUD guides you through every step (**Figure 8.38**). Notice, too, that once you've assigned a job to each part of the vertical scroll bar, the green rectangle has moved up to the top of the black track, so it can be ready to scroll whatever you tell it to scroll. Save the file and keep it open.

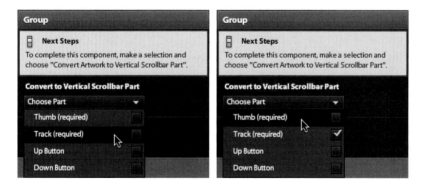

Figure 8.38 The HUD guides you through assigning the functions of Track and Thumb to the two small rectangles that constitute the vertical scroll bar.

6. Now you'll introduce the scroll bar to the text frame. Using the Breadcrumbs bar, return to the main project window. Select the scroll bar, and Shift-click to select the text frame next to it. The HUD perks up yet again. Click Choose Component, and select Scroll Panel from the list of options. The HUD prompts you to indicate which object contains the content to be scrolled. Click Edit Parts to enter the component editing mode. Once there, select the text frame and, under Convert Scroll Panel Part, click Choose Part. From the options, choose Scrolling Content (Required).

7. Using the Breadcrumbs bar, return to the main project window and test your project. Does the scroll bar cause the text to scroll up and down in the Web browser? Isn't this easy?

Creating the Pages/States This project will have four pages/states (**Figure 8.39**):

- The welcome screen

- Mad River Valley

- Green Mountains

- Llama Farm

Figure 8.39 The four Vermont pages/states.

You'll modify the current state of the project for the welcome screen, create three new pages/states for the other three topics, and set up navigation buttons.

1. In the Pages/States panel, rename Page1 **Home**. Click the Duplicate State button to duplicate the page, and name the new page **MadRiver**. Create another duplicate and name it **GreenMtns**, and one more duplicate, named **Llama**. Return to the **Home** page/state.

2. You'll create the **Mad River** button first. Unlock the **Buttons** layer, click the triangle to the left of the **Mad River** layer, and unlock all the objects in the **Mad River** layer, if necessary, by clicking the padlock icon for each sublayer. Rather than Shift-clicking the button components, you'll use an easier method: Just click the **Mad River** layer name, and all the objects on that layer are selected. Make sure that both the rounded rectangle and the text label are selected; otherwise, the area of the label becomes a "dead spot" in the middle of the button, which won't respond to clicking. In the HUD, click Choose Component and select Button from the list of options.

3. In the Interactions panel, choose Play Transition to State, and choose the **MadRiver** page/state. The button artwork already has a glow that was applied in Illustrator; you'll turn it off for the Up state of the button. Select the Up option in the HUD, then reselect the **Mad River** button when you enter component editing mode (you can tell you're in component editing mode when all other elements are grayed out, allowing you to work only on the current object). Scroll to the bottom of the Properties panel until you can see the Filters section. Click the Disable icon (⊗) to the right

of the word "Glow" (it's some distance away, and easy to overlook). This turns off the glow when the button is in the Up (default) state, but leaves the glow on in other states. Notice that Flash Catalyst recognizes the glow created in Illustrator, so you don't have to recreate the glow in Flash Catalyst. However, you might also notice that the glow is much more subdued as it's rendered in Flash Catalyst. You may decide that you have more control over such effects if you create them in Flash Catalyst.

4. Use the Breadcrumbs bar to return to the main project window, and save the file. Using the same techniques that you used for the **Mad River** button, set up the buttons for the **GreenMtns** and **Llama** pages/states. Save the file and keep it open.

5. Now you'll work on the three location pages/states. Select the **MadRiver** page/state. Turn on the visibility of the **photos** layer and unlock the layer. The layer contains a single image with three photos side by side in a horizontal strip. You'll move the strip to position each photo in the window now occupied by the pastel leaf art. Select the photo strip in the artboard, hold down Shift (to constrain the vertical movement of the image), and move the photo strip to the left until the **river** photograph is centered in the opening in the gray rectangle. Zoom in so you can check the position of the photo. Don't worry about the rest of the photo strip hanging awkwardly outside the main artboard. Because it's not within the confines of the artboard dimensions, the extra image content won't appear in the exported project.

6. Now you'll display text that provides information about the Mad River Valley. In the Layers panel, turn on the visibility of the **ghost block** layer (this provides a backdrop for the text), and the **Mad River Valley text** layer. If necessary, turn off the visibility of the **Grn Mtn** Text and **Llama farm text** layers.

7. Select the **GreenMtns** page/state. Turn on the **ghost block** layer. Turn off the **Mad River Valley text** and **Llama farm text** layers, and turn on the **Grn Mtn Text** layer. Slide the photo to the left to reveal the **valley** photo in the center window.

8. Select the **Llama** page/state. Turn on the **ghost block** layer. Turn *off* the **Mad River Valley** and **Grn Mtn Text** layers, and turn on the **Llama farm text** layer. Slide the photo to the left to reveal the llama photo in the center window. See? You start to develop a rhythm as you create the pages/states.

9. The llama text contains a hyperlink. Well, it isn't a hyperlink yet, but you'll fix that. Zoom in on the text in the ghost box area, switch to the Text tool, and select the blue text **www.vtllamas.com**. Copy the text to the Clipboard so you can use the URL in the next step.

10. You can't apply a Go To URL interaction directly to text, so you'll cheat. Select the llama text frame with the Select tool, and convert it to a button. In the Interactions panel, choose Go To URL (hidden under the default Play Transition to State entry). In the empty field below the Go To URL option, paste the text from the Clipboard. The field should now read **www.vtllamas.com**. In the pull-down below the URL field, choose Open in New Window (this opens a fresh browser window rather than replacing the current contents of the viewer's browser). Click OK and save the file. Test the project in the browser.

Adding Transitions and Sounds   As a final touch, you'll add smooth transitions to the sliding strip of photos, and import a short MP3 recording of rushing water to accompany any transitions to the **Mad River** page/state.

1. Select all the transitions in the transitions list at the left end of the Timelines panel. Click the triangle to the right of the Smooth Transition bar at the bottom of the Timelines panel to display the transition options. Use the following settings and click OK.

   - **Duration:** 1.5 seconds (so the images slide sedately into position)

   - **Timing:** Simultaneous

   - **Overwrite existing effects:** yes

2. To import a sound into the project, choose File > Import > Video/Sound File. Navigate to the **Importing Illustrator** folder and select **riversound.mp3**. This is a 4-second snippet of water sounds. The sound is not placed anywhere in the artboard of the project; it's added to the Library so you can invoke it when you need it (**Figure 8.40**). The Library panel is tucked in behind the Layers panel. Just click the Library tab to bring it to the front so you can view its contents.

A small bar at the bottom of the Timelines panel provides controls for adding an action, removing or modifying transitions, and scaling the timeline's time ruler (**Figure 8.41**). It's easy to overlook these controls; they're sort of hiding in plain sight.

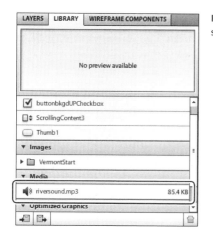

Figure 8.40 All assets are stored in the Library.

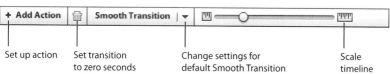

| Set up action | Set transition to zero seconds | Change settings for default Smooth Transition | Scale timeline |

Figure 8.41 The timeline controls let you add actions to transitions (such as sounds), remove transitions, change transition defaults, and scale the timeline display.

3. To trigger the river sound, you'll modify all transitions that take the viewer to the **MadRiver** page/state (don't panic; there are only three transitions to work on). Select the Home > MadRiver transition in the list of transitions to display its settings. In the Timelines window, select the entry for the **ThreeScenesAcross.psd** file (click the name rather than the duration slider). At the bottom of the Timelines panel, click the Add Action button and choose the Sound Effect option. The Select Asset dialog appears (**Figure 8.42**), displaying only the sound assets (you only have one, so you can't miss). The **riversound.mp3** asset is highlighted; all you have to do is click OK.

Figure 8.42 The Select Asset dialog allows you to select any asset that's already in the project Library. Since you've requested a sound effect, it's polite enough to highlight the Media assets to make it easy for you.

4. All the transitions are set to a duration of 1.5 seconds, but the river sound is 4 seconds long. You'll extend the duration of the sound's allotted time so it can play in its entirety, without getting stopped abruptly. In the timeline, select the duration bar for the sound, and either drag its pull handle to the right until you snap to the 4 second mark or see "Duration: 4s" in the tool tip that follows you as you pull. Alternatively, you can just type the value in the Properties panel (**Figure 8.43**). Although the sound lasts longer than the transition of the photograph, it will fade out as the viewer is reading the text describing the Mad River area of Vermont. Test the project. You should be accustomed to using Command-Return (Mac) or Control-Enter (Windows) by now.

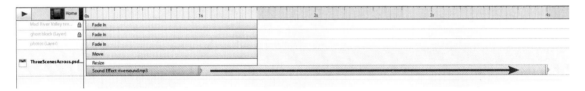

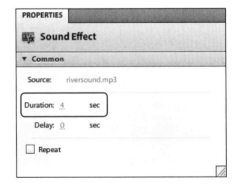

Figure 8.43 You can adjust the duration of the sound (or any transition) by dragging the pull handle of the duration slider in the timeline, or by typing a value in the Properties panel.

5. Now, fix the other two transitions to the **MadRiver** page/state:

   - GreenMtns > MadRiver

   - Llama > MadRiver

   Remember that you can preview any transition without having to test the project in a browser; just click the Play button at the top left of the timeline. Save the file and keep it open.

Round-Tripping to Illustrator   Since the drawing and editing tools are somewhat limited in Flash Catalyst, you'll be glad to know that you can round-trip most content. If you've imported Photoshop content, that content can be round-tripped to Photoshop. Illustrator content is, of course, round-tripped to Illustrator. You'll have more flexibility with Illustrator content, but there are still some slight limitations to what you can get away with:

- You can round-trip buttons, check boxes, and other named components, but you cannot round-trip objects that have been designated as custom/generic components (used when you want an object within the artboard to have multiple states of its own) unless you right-click (Mac: Control-click) and then choose Edit Component to take the object into Isolation Mode. In Isolation Mode, you can then select the object, right-click, and choose Edit in Adobe Photoshop CS5 or Edit in Adobe Illustrator CS5, whichever is appropriate.

- You can edit only one component at a time (but that component can be a group with multiple objects inside it).

- If the object is shared to multiple states, editing applies to all states.

- If an object appears in multiple pages/states (but does not itself have multiple states), you'll have to set it to be the same in all states after you return the edited content to Flash Catalyst (more about that below).

- While you're editing in Illustrator or Photoshop, you can see surrounding objects, which are grayed out for reference. But you cannot select or edit them.

1. In the Layers panel, unlock the **Title** layer and select the name of the layer to target all the objects in the layer (this is often much easier than Shift-clicking individual shapes). The title, **Scenic Vermont**, is selected in the artboard. Choose Modify > Edit in Adobe Illustrator CS5, or just right-click (Mac: Control-click) to choose that option from the contextual menu. An information alert is displayed (**Figure 8.44**), but if Illustrator is already running, the switch to Illustrator is so fast you may not see the alert. That's unfortunate, because it's giving you some good advice. You'd be tempted to choose File > Save in Illustrator when you're through fixing the content, but you need to click a subtle "Done" control instead. So take a good look at it here, preserved for your viewing pleasure.

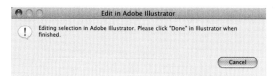

Figure 8.44 In a fleeting alert, Flash Catalyst advises you how to finish your editing session in Illustrator and return the edited content to Flash Catalyst.

2. In Illustrator, click one of the letters in the title text (it's no longer text; it was converted to outlines when the original Illustrator file was created). Open the Color panel (Window > Color), and choose RGB from the panel menu for the color mode. Adjust the sliders or type in these values: **R140-G200-B100**, a nice mossy green. If you're using the default Essentials workspace in Illustrator, the Color panel may be covering up the one control you need next. Close the Color panel, if necessary, so you can see the subtle options at the upper right of the document window (**Figure 8.45**). Click the word "Done" to save the edits. In the dialog that appears after you click Done, just click OK to accept the default settings (who are we to question?) and return the edited content to Flash Catalyst, updating your project.

Figure 8.45 Could it be more subtle? Click Done to save your edits in Illustrator and return to the Flash Catalyst project.

NOTE: In order to round-trip image content between Flash Catalyst and Photoshop or Photoshop Extended, you'll need to install the Flash Catalyst CS5 FXG Roundtrip Extension for Photoshop CS5. You can download the extension from the Adobe website here: http://labs.adobe.com/technologies/photoshopcs5_fxg.

3. Ah, but take a quick look at the other pages/states. The title is still white! Don't worry—you don't have to edit the title for each page/state. Just select States > Make Same in All Other States, or right-click (Mac: Control-click) and choose that option from the contextual menu. Now the title is green in all the pages/states, much like Vermont itself.

Take a look at the finished project (**Figure 8.46**). Even though this is probably new territory for you, think about what you've accomplished. You've started with an Illustrator file that wasn't overly complex (just well organized, if I do say so myself), and you've created a presentation with sliding transitions and a babbling brook—all without writing a single line of code. You should be proud. More than that, you should be inspired to dig deeper into the fun you can have in Flash Catalyst.

Figure 8.46 The four pages of the Vermont project.

Chapter 9

Putting It All Together

Now that you've been exposed to the tools and functions in Adobe Photoshop, Adobe Illustrator, Adobe InDesign, and Adobe Flash Professional, it's time to put it all together. In this chapter you'll explore concepts more deeply as you revisit topics that were introduced in previous chapters.

In this chapter's exercises, you'll be presented with an InDesign document that was originally intended for print. You'll modify its dimensions and massage its content into an appropriate format for onscreen viewing. You'll create buttons in Photoshop, and you'll import Illustrator artwork into Flash Professional to create a simple animation and export it as a SWF. You'll combine all the pieces in InDesign and export the whole shebang to SWF, sit back and admire it, and pat yourself on the back.

NOTE: If you're using InDesign's Live Preflight feature with settings appropriate for print, you may notice the red light in the lower-left corner of the document window, indicating preflight errors (mainly RGB images). The print document in the exercises is not fully print-compliant. Please ignore the errors; they'll be irrelevant when the file is exported to SWF.

Analyzing the InDesign Print Document

If you're creating an ad campaign for a client, and you know that you will need to create both print and Web versions, you may have an advantage. If you can persuade your client that a landscape format is way cooler than the stodgy old portrait format, you're ahead of the game. Start with a horizontal format, and it's much easier for you to repurpose your print content for Web use.

If you're unable to convince your client of the wisdom and appeal of a chic horizontal format, you'll have considerably more work massaging your text and graphics into the new dimensions. Let's take a look at just how challenging that might be. You'll open a magazine article for a fictional resort and rework it for onscreen viewing.

1. Launch InDesign CS5. Navigate to the **Ch_9_Exercises** > **InDesign Rework** folder, and open **OutdoorMagForPrint.indd**. This document is set up for traditional print. It's 8.5 by 11 inches, vertical format (**Figure 9.1**). In order to prepare it for onscreen viewing, you could take screen shots, distort them in Photoshop, and... nah, that would be cheating (and ugly). You should do it the Right Way.

Figure 9.1 The vertical format of a traditional print piece isn't appropriate for onscreen viewing. But you can use a print document as a starting point for a Web document—with a little help from InDesign.

2. The Right Way involves InDesign's great Layout Adjustment feature, which gives you some help during the process of changing your document's dimensions. In essence, you give InDesign permission to massage your content according to the rules you specify. To use this feature while you

change the print version of the magazine document to Web-appropriate dimensions, choose Layout > Layout Adjustment (**Figure 9.2**). Usually the default options will give you reasonable results; all you have to do is check the option to Enable Layout Adjustment. Examine the options that the Layout Adjustment dialog offers for allowing graphics and groups to resize. The option to allow ruler guides to move means that objects that are snapped to those guides will move along with the guides (including margin guides, if you change the margin settings), which helps preserve as much of your document's layout as possible. Ignoring object and layer locks means that nothing gets left behind while other objects are being repositioned. Understandably, the less drastically the document's dimensions are changed, the less cleanup work you have to do. Click OK. Nothing changes in your document yet.

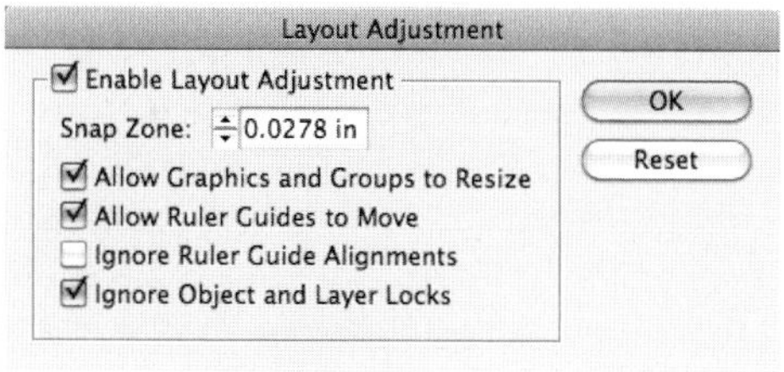

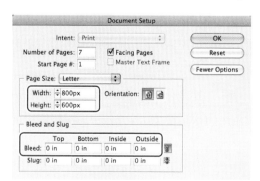

Figure 9.2 The Layout Adjustment dialog lets you solicit InDesign's help in changing the dimensions of a document.

3. You've given InDesign permission to massage your document layout. Now you have to change the document dimensions. Before you do, choose File > Save As, and save the document as **OutdoorMagWebNew.indd** in the **InDesign Rework** folder. Choose File > Document Setup (**Figure 9.3**). Because the document began life as a print document, InDesign doesn't allow you to just change the document intent to Web, but there are workarounds. In the Width field, type **800 px**, and change the Height value to **600 px**. InDesign immediately converts the measurements to inches, but that doesn't matter. Set the bleed value to 0, and click OK.

Figure 9.3 Even though the document is not currently using the pixel measurement system, you can still type values in pixels in the Document Setup dialog.

NOTE: If you'd like a peek into the future, the finished InDesign file is in **Ch_9_Exercises > Finished Files > InDesign File**.

The final SWF and HTML files are in **Ch_9_Exercises > Finished Files > Web Files**.

4. Yikes! What a mess (**Figure 9.4**). But it's still (usually) better than starting over. At least all the text and graphics are in the layout. They just need to be moved around and modified to work in the new page orientation.

Figure 9.4 A drastic change in dimensions can result in a real mess, even with the assistance of Layout Adjustment features. But it often beats starting from scratch.

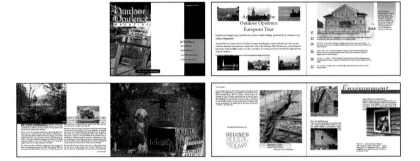

5. Experiment with the resized file's contents. The images weren't high-res to begin with; if they were all 300 ppi for best results in printing, the exercise files would be pretty hefty. They were downsampled to save space on the exercise disc (and your hard drive). But now that the project is going to be used for onscreen viewing, that's no longer an issue. You don't have to completely redo the file; you'll just modify it until you get a sense of what would be involved if this were a live project for which you were billing a client. In actual production, you'll have to remember to factor in the time you'll need to spend repurposing print content for Web deployment. Once you've poked around in the file, save and close it. There's already a modified file for you to use as you continue in this chapter. In the **InDesign Rework** folder, open **OutdoorMagForWeb.indd** (**Figure 9.5**). Before you start working on the file, save it as **MagForWebNew.indd** in the **InDesign Rework** folder. Keep the file open.

Figure 9.5 The provided **OutdoorMagForWeb.indd** file shows you how print content was modified to fit the horizontal page and new dimensions.

6. To ensure that any transparent effects (such as soft edges or drop shadows) render correctly in the RGB color space that will be used during export to SWF, choose Edit > Transparency Blend Space > Document RGB. For consistent color conversion during export to SWF, you'll need to change your Color Settings. Choose Edit > Color Settings, and switch to North America Web/Internet (**Figure 9.6**)—but don't forget to change back to your normal color management settings when you finish the Web project.

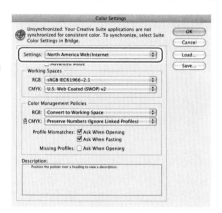

Figure 9.6 Since InDesign will convert all content to sRGB, consider changing your Color Settings to North America Web/Internet for more reliable conversion and onscreen viewing.

7. Examine the Swatches panel (Window > Swatches). If this project were destined for print, the multiple spot colors, as well as any non-CMYK colors, would have to be resolved. Good news: All swatches, regardless of species, will be rendered to sRGB during export to SWF, so you don't need to worry about their current flavor. However (and this is even more good news), since swatches will be rendered as sRGB during export to SWF, you might want to change their recipes to RGB and brighten them up, since you're no longer limited by the smaller CMYK gamut.

8. Before you do any more work on the magazine document, take a quick look at the SWF export dialog. Choose File > Export and select the Flash Player (SWF) format. Navigate to the **InDesign Rework** folder, and name the export **MagPageTest.swf**. Examine the settings in the export dialog. There are no options for "spread" or "single pages." Make sure Paper Color and Interactive Page Curl are checked. Click OK to complete the export, and view the exported SWF in a browser (or Flash Player). The two-page spreads are intact, and now that the document is in a horizontal format, you have to scroll a bit to find the edge of the page. Now you know: InDesign's export to SWF keeps spreads intact.

TIP: When you repurpose a print document for onscreen viewing, consider increasing text size to enhance readability. And keep in mind that sans-serif fonts are often more legible than serif fonts, especially at smaller sizes. Since changing font style and size can profoundly alter your layout, anticipate this when you're designing a piece that will be used for both print and Web.

9. The pages of the magazine are formatted to fit on the screen, but only one at a time. You'll have to separate the two-page spreads into single pages, but it's not obvious how you can convince InDesign to let you do that. Go ahead, try it. By default, if you delete a page from a spread, the next page in the document shuffles up to take its place. InDesign doesn't allow an empty spot. Open the Pages panel (Window > Pages), and notice that Allow Document Pages to Shuffle is on by default (**Figure 9.7**). Turn off that option so you can separate the pages.

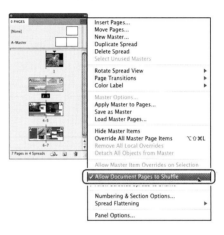

Figure 9.7 Disabling the Allow Document Pages to Shuffle option allows you to pull spreads apart into separate pages. It also allows you to glue pages together however you'd like.

10. Click and drag page 3 to the right far enough that you see a black vertical bar (**Figure 9.8**). If you don't drag far enough, the page won't be dislodged. Pull pages 5 and 7 loose using the same method, and then save the file.

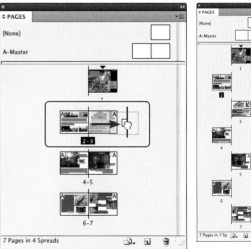
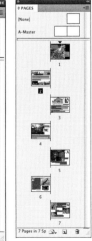

Figure 9.8 Once you've disabled the Shuffle option, you can pull the spreads apart into individual pages. Just pull far enough away from the spread that you see a black vertical bar.

11. Rather than export to SWF to check your work, test your file in the Preview panel (Window > Interactive > Preview). Choose Edit Preview Settings from the Preview panel menu, and turn off the option to Include Interactive Page Curl (it will get in the way of testing in later steps). Drag the corner of the Preview panel to make it big enough so you can see content at a reasonable size. Set the mode to Preview Document (). Refresh the preview by clicking the Play button ( ), then page through the magazine using the navigation controls in the Preview panel. Save the file and keep it open so you can start bringing it to life.

Adding Hyperlinks

Since this document is just an excerpt from a magazine, you'll have to create only a few hyperlinks to help out the viewer. If you had to manually create hyperlinks for the entire 64-page magazine, that would be painful and time consuming. Keep that in mind when you're planning a project that will be used for print and Web. Get in the habit of building hyperlinks and cross-references as you go. It's easier when you do that task during the flow of production, and it's likely to be less error prone.

Hyperlinks intended to lead a viewer from one page to another within a document can be created with one of four methods:

- You can designate selected text (or an object) as a hyperlink destination, and create a hyperlink to jump to that destination. This method requires two constituents: the destination, and the hyperlink that takes the viewer to the destination.

- You can use the Page Anchor option to attach a hyperlink to any text or object, and direct it to jump to any page in the document. In this method, there's no need to create a hyperlink destination first; all you have to do is specify the page to be targeted.

- You can establish a cross-reference relationship between a hyperlink and a text target within the document. In this method, the target text must be tagged with a specified paragraph style (that's how InDesign "finds" it).

- A Text Anchor allows you to select any text as a target, name that target, and establish a hyperlink that jumps to the target. The hyperlink "trigger" can be any object or selected text. The advantage of this method is that it isn't dependent on paragraph styles, and it retains the hyperlink relationship even if the target or hyperlink trigger is moved.

And there's a fifth type of hyperlink. A URL hyperlink takes the viewer to a Web address when clicked. In this project, you'll use both the Page Anchor and Text Anchor methods of creating hyperlinks and hyperlink destinations. You'll also create hyperlinks to lead the viewer to fictional online resources.

1. Choose Window > Workspace > Interactive to bring up all the necessary panels. First, you'll create two URL hyperlinks, which will take the viewer to the Web. Go to page 2 of the document. Open the Hyperlinks panel (Window > Interactive > Hyperlinks). In the last line of text, use the Type tool to select just the text **www.outdooropulencemag.com/tour**. Choose the Underline option (**T**)in the Control panel, or use the keyboard shortcut: Command-Shift-U (Mac) or Ctrl-Shift-U (Windows). Keep the underlined text selected, and open the Color panel (Window > Color > Color). In the Color panel menu, choose RGB to switch to the RGB color space, and drag the B (blue) slider all the way to the right until the value is 255. (Show a viewer some underlined blue text, and they will feel irresistibly compelled to click it.) Click the New Swatch icon () at the bottom of the Swatches panel (Window > Color > Swatches) to add the new blue swatch. Double-click the swatch, uncheck the Name With Color Value option, and name it **Hyperlink**. You'll need it again.

2. The text *looks* like a hyperlink; now you'll make it behave like one. With the text still selected, choose New Hyperlink From URL from the Hyperlinks panel menu. InDesign recognizes the URL format and automatically vacuums up the text, without you having to retype the Web address (**Figure 9.9**). Perform a test export to SWF to make sure the hyperlink is clickable. Since you're viewing the file locally, Flash Player displays a security alert telling you that it's stopped a potentially unsafe operation. You may remember from Chapter 2 that you'd have to change the Flash Player settings to allow this—and that it's not usually a good idea to do so. At this point, you're exporting the project to SWF just to test whether the hyperlink is active, so don't change your settings.

Figure 9.9 InDesign recognizes text in a URL format when you create a hyperlink from selected text.

3. Go to page 6 of the magazine. Select the text **www.helenehideaway.com**, and choose **New Hyperlink From URL** from the Hyperlinks panel menu. If you have trouble selecting the hyperlink text, temporarily switch to the Selection tool by holding down Command (Mac) or Ctrl (Windows) and clicking the text; this will target the small text frame containing the hyperlink text. Release the Command or Ctrl key, and you should now be able to select the text. The text is already blue and underlined, but the blue is a bit dull. Apply the Hyperlink swatch you created in Step 1. Save the file and keep it open.

4. Now you'll create several hyperlinks to help viewers find and follow an article in the magazine. First, you'll create a hyperlink destination (a place for the viewer to land), then the hyperlink trigger that takes them to the destination. Go to page 4 of the magazine, where the Helene's Hideaway article begins. Use the Type tool to select the headline **From Brunch In The Garden...** and choose **New Hyperlink Destination** from the Hyperlinks panel menu. Choose Text Anchor for the destination type. By default, InDesign names the destination based on the selected text. Change the hyperlink name to **Article Start** (**Figure 9.10**). Notice that the hyperlink destination does not appear in the Hyperlinks panel. You'll have to accept this; you'll only see evidence of hyperlink destinations when you create the hyperlink that will go searching for them.

Figure 9.10 It's a good idea to change the name of a Text Anchor hyperlink destination so you'll recognize it later when you're creating the hyperlink that connects to it.

5. Now you'll create the hyperlink that jumps to the beginning of the article. Go to page 3 of the magazine, which contains the Table of Contents. With the Type tool, select the first entry in the TOC (**04—This Month...**). You can quadruple-click in the paragraph to select the entire paragraph without having to click and drag. Once the paragraph is selected, choose New Hyperlink from the Hyperlinks panel menu. Choose **Text Anchor** for the Link To option. Since there's currently only one text anchor in the document, you can't go wrong. **Article Start** should already be selected in the Text Anchor pull-down menu. Don't click OK quite yet. You should explore the options in the New Hyperlink dialog.

6. Besides letting you pick the target for the hyperlink, the New Hyperlink dialog (**Figure 9.11**) also gives you control of the appearance and behavior of the hyperlink itself. Notice that you can select a character style to apply to the selected hyperlink text (great when you want to call attention to a hyperlink created from just a word or phrase, rather than the entire paragraph). At the bottom of the dialog, the Appearance options let you specify whether the hot spot area is indicated with a visible rectangle (the default is Invisible Rectangle). If you choose the Visible Rectangle option, the Color, Width, and Style options come to life. The Highlight option governs the visual feedback that viewers receive when they click. You can choose from None, Invert, Outline, and Inset. The None option does, well, nothing. The Invert option momentarily turns the area of the hyperlink to a negative as the viewer clicks. The Outline option displays a stroke around the clicked area, and the Inset option indents the hyperlink area into the page, like a pushed button. For this project, just leave the appearance settings at Invisible Rectangle, with None for the highlight.

Figure 9.11 The Appearance options give you control over how the hyperlink hot spot area appears, and how it responds when clicked.

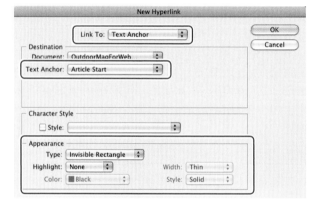

Creating Jumpline Hyperlinks

In a printed piece, *jumplines* (also called continuation lines) are used to lead the reader through an article that continues across multiple pages. You don't have to keep track of the pages containing a story; InDesign automatically does that for you. First, you'll set up the jumplines, and then you'll create the hyperlinks and their destinations so the viewer can follow the article about Helene's Holistic Hideaway.

1. Go to page 4 of the magazine. Underneath the story text is the small text frame that will become the jumpline. Choose the Type tool, then click at the end of the text. Press the spacebar to add a space after the word "page"

(it won't look as if the space has been added, but hang on). Right-click (Mac: Control-click) and choose **Insert Special Character** > **Markers** > **Next Page Number**. This inserts the code InDesign uses to keep track of the article. Initially, it will read "continued on page 4," because it can't currently communicate with the frame containing the article.

2. Press the Escape key to switch to the Selection tool, and move the small text frame up until it touches the bottom edge of the article text frame. And *voilà* (which is French for "jumpline"), the text now reads "continued on page 6."

3. While jumplines help readers of a printed piece, viewers of interactive documents need something they can click. A hyperlink can be attached to either selected text or the frame containing the text. The difference is the size of the clickable area created. If you attach the hyperlink to selected text, only the small area of the text is clickable. If you attach the hyperlink to the text frame, the entire area of the frame is "live." There are advantages to each. In a busy page, limiting the clickable area to just a line of text might be helpful, but the larger area of the containing frame is an easier target. In this document, you'll attach the jumpline hyperlinks to the text frames rather than selected text. With the jumpline frame still selected, choose New Hyperlink from the Hyperlinks panel menu. Choose Page for the Link To option, and enter **6** for the page number. Leave the other settings at their defaults, and click OK.

4. Go to page 6 to fix the other jumpline. At the top of the page, click after the text in the small jumpline frame. Press the spacebar and then right-click and choose **Insert Special Character** > **Markers** > **Previous Page Number**. Switch to the Selection tool and move the frame down so it touches the top edge of the article text frame. The jumpline text should now read "continued from page 4."

5. Create a new hyperlink for the jumpline text frame on page 6, following the instructions in Step 3 above, setting the page target to page 4 so the viewer can jump back to the earlier part of the article. You can close the Hyperlinks panel for now.

6. Test your file in the Preview panel, using the navigation controls at the bottom of the panel to go to page 3 of the magazine (since you disabled the page curl). Test the hyperlink you created in the Table of Contents; it should take you to page 4. Test the jumpline hyperlink; it should take you to page 6. Test the jumpline hyperlink on page 6 to make sure it takes you back to page 4. Save the file and keep it open (or take a break).

Multistate Objects: Creating a Slideshow

Creating an interactive version of a project can open the doors to including more content that wouldn't fit in the confines of a printed version. In this magazine, it would be nice to show even more scenes for the Outdoor Opulence European tour, without having to make the images smaller. You'll use a multistate object to create a slideshow, and control it with buttons.

To make room for new, larger images, you would have to completely redesign page 2. Rather than make you do that, I've included some replacement content as InDesign snippets. A *snippet* is just a record of page geometry, and can be used to store text and graphic frames—even entire pages. Snippets don't include graphics, just references to them. (However, if graphics are embedded in a document, they will be embedded in the snippets exported from the document.)

1. Before you proceed with the remodeling job, save the file at its current state.

2. Go to page 2 of the magazine. Select and delete all the frames containing images, then move the text frame up to the top margin of the page (**Figure 9.12**) to make room for the slideshow you'll create.

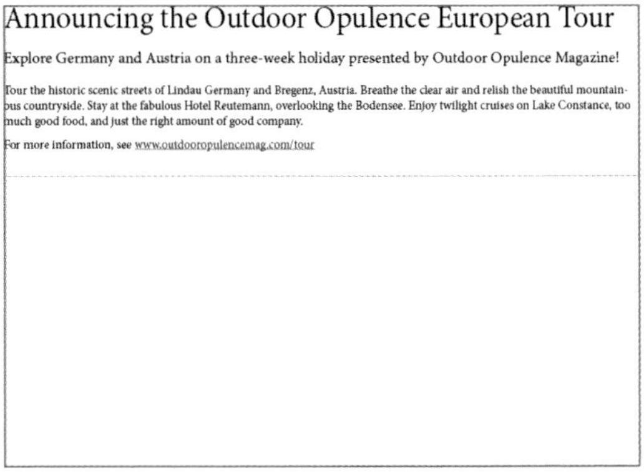

Figure 9.12 Reposition the text frame so the image slideshow can be placed below it.

Announcing the Outdoor Opulence European Tour

Explore Germany and Austria on a three-week holiday presented by Outdoor Opulence Magazine!

Tour the historic scenic streets of Lindau Germany and Bregenz, Austria. Breathe the clear air and relish the beautiful mountainous countryside. Stay at the fabulous Hotel Reutemann, overlooking the Bodensee. Enjoy twilight cruises on Lake Constance, too much good food, and just the right amount of good company.

For more information, see www.outdooropulencemag.com/tour

3. Now you'll bring in the images for the slideshow, the buttons to control the slideshow, and a caption, all as InDesign snippets. First you'll bring in the images. Choose File > Place, navigate to the **Ch_9_Exercises > InDesign Rework > SlideShowImages** folder and select **SlideShowImages.idms**. Check the Links panel (Window > Links) to make sure the image links are current. Because the snippet was created on my computer, it remembers the original location of the images. If necessary, relink all the images. The

image frames are offset so you can see how many there are (**Figure 9.13**), and to make it easier to select all frames for subsequent steps. Keep the frames selected for the next step.

Figure 9.13 The snippet for the images contains all the page-geometry information to create frames and link to images.

4. Align the top and left edges of the selected frames (**Figure 9.14**), and be careful to keep the frames selected. If you do accidentally deselect, marquee-select the aligned frames by clicking and dragging across a corner of the assembly to reselect them (you don't have to completely surround the frames; just snag a portion). Resist the temptation to group the frames. You're going to create a multistate object out of the ten selected frames. If you group the frames, this won't work.

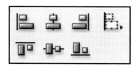

Figure 9.14 Align the top and left edges of the selected image frames, being careful not to deselect them.

5. With the frames still selected, open the Object States panel (Window > Interactive > Object States), and click the Convert Selection to Multistate Object icon ( ) at the bottom of the panel. Name the new multistate object **tour slides** (**Figure 9.15**).

Figure 9.15 Each selected image frame becomes a state in the multistate object.

6. In the Object States panel, select the state you'd like for the initial view (we used State 7). Center the object horizontally in the page (Smart Guides will help), and position the bottom edge just above the bottom margin guide. Now you'll bring in the caption and the button art. Choose File > Place, navigate back to the **Ch_9_Exercises** > **InDesign Rework** > **SlideShowImages** folder, select **Caption.idms**, and Command-click (Windows) or Control-click (Mac) to select **SlideShowButtons.idms**, then select Open. Click once to place the caption, and click again to place the buttons (they're not buttons yet, but soon will be).

7. Position the caption text frame below the slideshow object, centered horizontally in the page. Then position the orange triangular buttons on either side of the slideshow object (**Figure 9.16**), aligning them vertically with each other, and center the buttons and slideshow object vertically so everything is nice and neat. Again, Smart Guides (View > Grids & Guides > Smart Guides) can help.

Figure 9.16 Center the multistate object below the text, and position the caption and triangular buttons as shown.

8. Open the Buttons panel (Window > Interactive > Buttons). Select the left-pointing orange triangle, and click the Convert Object to a Button icon ( ) at the bottom of the Buttons panel. Name the button **prev**. For Event, choose On Release, and click the plus sign by Actions to choose Go To Previous State. The **tour slides** multistate object is the only likely target in the page, so its name automatically appears.

9. Using Step 8 as a guide, set up the right triangle to be a button named **next** that will take the viewer to the next state of the tour slides. Test the project in the Preview panel, and save the file. Next, you'll create some navigation buttons in Photoshop, so you'll be leaving InDesign for a while. If you like, close down InDesign while you're working in Photoshop.

Photoshop: Making Buttons

You need to provide navigation buttons in the online version of the magazine so viewers can move from page to page. As you saw when you were creating the slideshow, you could just create InDesign objects and convert them to buttons. But for this magazine, you'll create some buttons in Photoshop so you can take advantage of layer comps.

1. Launch Photoshop. Choose File > New. Set the width and height to 1 inch. Set the resolution to 300 ppi, the color mode to RGB, and the background to Transparent. Name the new file **PrevPage.psd**. While the buttons will be much smaller when you place them in the interactive magazine project, it's easier to see the results of effects while working at a larger size.

2. To create the **PrevPage** art, you'll use a vector shape. Select the Custom Shape Tool, hidden under the Rectangle Tool (**Figure 9.17**).

Figure 9.17 To start hunting for a vector shape to use as the basis for the **prevpage** button, choose the Custom Shape Tool.

3. In the Options bar at the top of the Photoshop interface, click the downward pointing triangle to display the currently available vector shapes. If you've modified your set of shapes, you may not see the same assortment as shown in **Figure 9.18**. Click the circle-in-a-triangle icon to access the panel menu, and choose Shapes from the list of preset assortments of vector art. An alert appears, asking if you want to replace the current shapes with the new set. Click OK if you want to replace the current set, or click Append if you want to keep the current set and add the new ones.

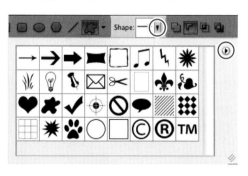

Figure 9.18 To explore the shapes included with Photoshop, access the panel menu of the Shapes panel.

4. Now that you have more shapes to play with, search for the hollow triangle shape (**Figure 9.19**). Select the shape, but don't start drawing in the image yet. In the Color panel (Window > Color), choose the RGB color mode from the panel menu and create a color that's **R245-G130-B32**, a medium orange.

Figure 9.19 Once you've loaded the additional shapes, find and select the hollow triangle shape.

Figure 9.20 The Shape Layers option allows you to create solid color layers with vector edges. Switch back to the plain old Paths option (center) when you're done.

NOTE: It's easy to forget you chose the Shape Layers option, and it will bite you the next time you intend to draw a plain old clipping path, insisting on creating a solid shape layer. Thus, some advice: When you're finished creating a Shape Layer, reselect the Paths option (the center of the three vector options in the Options bar).

5. Before you start creating the shape, change the mode used for vector content by choosing the Shape Layers option in the Options bar (**Figure 9.20**). Instead of creating a nonprinting path, this mode allows you to create solid color layers with vector masks.

6. Start near the upper-left corner of the image, hold down Shift to constrain the shape, and drag diagonally to create the orange hollow triangle, leaving enough room for a glow you'll create later. Switch to the Path Selection tool (🔾), and reposition the triangle in the center of the image. Look in the Layers panel (Window > Layers); the layer consists of a sheet of solid orange, masked by the vector triangle shape (**Figure 9.21**). One of the advantages of using a vector shape layer is that you can edit the shape with path editing tools such as the Pen tool and the Direct Selection tool (white arrow). For example, if you want to tweak the position of the triangle in the image, just use the Path Selection tool to move it. To rotate the image so the triangle points to the left, choose **Image > Image Rotation > 90° CCW**. Choose File > Save and save the image in the **Ch_9_Exercises > Photoshop Buttons** folder as **PrevPage.psd** (you named the file as you created it, so you shouldn't have to rename it).

Figure 9.21 Note that a vector mask looks a bit different in the Layers panel, to differentiate it from a pixel-based layer mask.

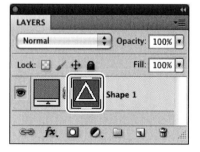

7. Click the Layer Style icon (*fx*) at the bottom of the Layers panel, and choose Bevel and Emboss. Use the settings shown in **Figure 9.22**.

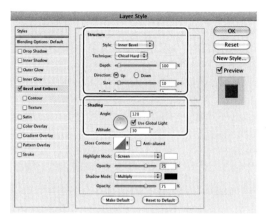

Figure 9.22 Use these settings for the **prevpage.psd** button. Leave all other values at the default settings:

Style: Inner Bevel

Technique: Chisel Hard

Depth: 100%

Direction: Up

Size: 10 px

Soften: 0 px

Angle: 120°

Altitude: 30°

Global Light: On

8. The current appearance of the triangle button will be the **Up** state. So you can invoke that state when you're creating a button, you'll store the current appearance in a layer comp. Open the Layer Comps panel (Window > Layer Comps), and click the New Layer Comp icon ( ). Name the layer comp **UP**, check the Visibility and Appearance options so those attributes will be stored in the layer comp, and click OK.

9. Now you'll modify the image for the **Over** button state. Click the Layer Style button at the bottom of the Layers panel, and choose the Outer Glow option. Use the settings shown in **Figure 9.23**. Create a new layer comp, named **OVER**.

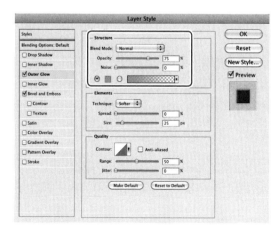

Figure 9.23 To create the Over appearance for the triangle button, use these settings, and leave the other values at their defaults:

Blend Mode: Normal

Opacity: 75%

Noise: 0%

Color: R255-G155-B60

Figure 9.24 The finished set of page buttons, with anatomically correct highlights and shadows.

10. Click in the small square to the left of the **UP** state in the Layer Comps panel to make that the default state of the image. Save the file and keep it open.

11. You could use this triangle for both the previous and next page buttons, but the highlight and shadow would be wrong on one of them. Yes, I know that's a little nitpicky. But it's quickly done, and then all of us nitpickers can sleep soundly. First you'll flip the artwork, then you'll move the sun to the correct position. Choose Image > Image Rotation > Flip Canvas Horizontal. In the Layers panel, double-click the entry for Bevel and Emboss, and change the Angle value to 120°. Save the file as **NextPage. psd** in the **Ch_9_Exercises** > **Photoshop Buttons** folder and keep it open for the next part of the exercise. Now you have a matching set of page buttons, with consistent highlights and shadows (**Figure 9.24**).

Importing Illustrator Artwork into Photoshop

For the Home button, you'll start with some existing Illustrator artwork and apply the same Bevel and Emboss layer style, as well as the orange glow, so all the buttons have a consistent appearance.

1. To avoid ruining the **NextPage** button, duplicate it before you begin changing it to create the Home button. Choose Image > Duplicate, and name the new image **HomeButton.psd**. Close the **NextPage.psd** image.

2. To bring in the Illustrator artwork, choose File > Place, navigate to the **Ch_9_Exercises** > **Photoshop Buttons** folder and select **Home Path.ai**. Make sure Crop To is set to Bounding Box, and click OK. The house artwork is imported and centered in the image. Note the handles around the art. This is because you've placed content. Photoshop gives you the opportunity to reposition or transform placed art before finalizing the import. The artwork just happens to fit (that happens in lesson files, but rarely in Real Life). Just press Return (Mac) or Enter (Windows) to commit to the import.

3. To duplicate the Bevel and Emboss settings for the original triangle button, hold down Option (Mac) or Alt (Windows), select the small **ƒx** to the right of the **Shape 1** layer (the triangle), and move it up to the **Home Path** layer. If you find this difficult to do (it can be stubborn to click in just the right spot), there's another method. Select the **Shape 1** layer and choose Layer > Layer Style > Copy Layer Style. Then select the **Home Path** layer and choose Layer > Layer Style > Paste Layer Style. Delete the **Shape 1** layer, save the file, and keep it open.

4. Look in the Layer Comps panel. Both of the layer comp entries have yellow warning triangles because the content to which they referred is gone. You'll keep the layer comp names, but make them represent the **UP** and **OVER** states of the new Home button. The current state of this image will constitute the **UP** state, so select the **UP** layer comp name in the Layer Comps panel (*don't* select the square to the left of the name; select the name itself). Then choose Update Layer Comp from the Layer Comps panel menu. The yellow warning triangle should disappear from the **UP** state.

5. Now you'll add the same orange glow that was used in the **OVER** states of the triangle page buttons. Click the Layer Style icon at the bottom of the Layers panel, and choose the Bevel and Emboss option. For Blend Mode, choose Normal, and change the Color to **R255-G155-B60**. Leave all other values at the default settings and click OK.

6. Select the **OVER** layer comp (again, click the layer comp name, not the square to the left of the name), and choose Update Layer Comp from the Layer Comps panel menu. The yellow warning triangle should disappear from the **OVER** state.

7. Click in the square to the left of the **UP** layer comp name to make it the default appearance of the image. Save the file as **HomeButton.psd** in the **Ch_9_Exercises** > **Photoshop Buttons** folder, and close the image (**Figure 9.25**).

You can close Photoshop now. It's time to return to InDesign so you can add and activate the new buttons.

Figure 9.25 The finished Home button, in its **UP** state.

Adding Navigation Buttons

You added navigation buttons in Chapter 2, so this should be old hat (or old button) for you. But if you want to streamline the process by placing the buttons on the master page, you'll have to further modify the document.

1. Launch InDesign and reopen **MagForWebNew.indd** in the **InDesign Rework** folder. Currently, the document still considers itself a facing-page document. All left-hand pages are based on the left master page, and all right-hand pages are based on the right master page. You could place the buttons twice (once on each master page), but there's an easier way. Choose **File** > **Document Setup**, and *uncheck* the **Facing Pages** option. Note that this can be tricky in documents with crossover elements, but that won't be an issue with this document.

2. In the **Pages** panel (Window > Pages), double-click the **A-Master** label in the top part of the panel. If you see a pair of text frames at the bottom of the pasteboard, delete them (they're leftover folio frames, and you don't need them in the interactive version of the magazine). From the Pages panel menu, choose Master Options for A-Master. In the dialog, change the number of pages to **1** (**Figure 9.26**) and click OK. Save the file and keep it open.

Figure 9.26 Once you've changed the Document Setup to Single Pages, change the number of pages in the A-Master to 1, so you only have to keep track of one master page.

3. When you place the button artwork, you want to make sure none of the buttons interfere with artwork already in the magazine pages. Wouldn't it be great if you could look at all the pages simultaneously to see the repercussions of positioning the buttons on the master page? You can— almost. Choose Window > Arrange > New Window, then choose Window > Arrange > Tile to place both views of the document side by side. This may seem like an instruction from the Department of Redundancy Department, but you'll soon see how handy this is when you're juggling master page content and document page objects.

4. Click in the right document window to make it the active window, and then double-click the thumbnail for Page 1 in the Pages panel. Click in the left document window to make it the active window, and then double-click the **A-Master** label. Double-check the windows before you proceed. You should see "A-Master" at the bottom-left of the left document window, and the numeral "1" at the bottom left of the right document window. As you work through the next few steps, remember: Master on the left, document on the right.

5. In the Layers panel, create a new top layer and name it **buttons**. Lock the **text** and **graphics** layers, and target the new **buttons** layer. In the right window (the document), reduce the magnification so you can see two or three pages if possible.

6. Once again, click in the left (master) window to make it active. Choose File > Place, navigate to the **Photoshop Buttons** folder, and select **PrevPage.psd**, **HomeButton.psd**, and **NextPage.psd**. Click to place the

three buttons under the bottom margin of the master page (**Figure 9.27**). Scale the buttons to 50% of their current size, and align their top edges using the alignment controls in the Control panel. Select all three buttons, and use the Distribute Horizontal Centers control (⬍) in the Control panel to distribute the buttons evenly. Save the file and keep it open.

Figure 9.27 Position the button artwork close together, with enough distance between them to avoid accidentally clicking the wrong one.

7. Click in the right window to make it active. Scroll through the right window to see what's happening throughout the document. If the buttons are too high in the master page, click in the left window to target the A-Master, and move the buttons down a bit. This won't fix all the pages; you'll have to modify pages 2 and 5.

8. The buttons don't show on the cover, because it's based on the None master. Double-click the page 1 thumbnail to target it, and Alt-click the thumbnail for the A-Master master page (Mac: Option-click the A-Master). This applies the A-Master page to page 1. You should now see the navigation buttons on the cover page.

9. Lock the **buttons** layer, and unlock the **text** and **graphics** layers. Go to page 2, and move the slideshow and caption text frame as far up as you can without crowding the text at the top of the page. Select the caption text below the slideshow, and reduce it to 20 points. Move the caption frame up until it clears the buttons by a comfortable margin.

10. Go to page 3, the Table of Contents. There's no room to move the Table of Contents text up without it being lost in the background image. Instead, you'll modify the paragraph style used by the text to reduce the space between paragraphs. Click in empty space to deselect anything that might be selected. In the Paragraph Styles panel (Window > Styles > Paragraph Styles), double-click **1_Blue TOC** to open the Style Options dialog. In the left column of the dialog, select Indents and Spacing and change the Space After value to **0.1875**. Click OK to exit the dialog.

11. On page 5, select and move the fireplace image and the text frames below the image up until they clear the navigation buttons.

12. If necessary, return to the A-Master page and reposition the buttons. As long as the bottom edge of the buttons is about 0.1 inch from the bottom

of the page, that should be satisfactory. Close one of the document windows; it doesn't matter which one (just don't close both). Save the file and keep it open.

Assigning Actions to the Navigation Buttons

Now that you've finally positioned the navigation buttons, it's time to add the actions. Once you've done that, you'll reposition or delete a few buttons in the document pages.

1. Double-click in the A-Master page to target it. Open the Buttons panel (Window > Interactive > Buttons). Using the methods you learned earlier, select the left triangle, convert it to a button, and name the button **PrevPage**. Click the plus sign by Actions and choose the Go To Previous Page action. Keep the button selected.

2. Select the Rollover state in the Buttons panel. Switch to the Direct Selection tool (white arrow) and click inside the button frame to select the image rather than the frame (if you're zoomed up sufficiently, you can just click the Content Grabber "donut" inside the frame to target the image). Choose Object > Object Layer Options. In the Object Layer Options dialog, choose the **OVER** layer comp and click OK.

3. Now you'll create the next page button. Select the right triangle, convert it to a button, and name the button **NextPage**. Add the Go To Next Page action. Select the Rollover state and use Object Layer Options to choose the **OVER** layer comp so the button will show an orange glow when the viewer rolls over it.

4. Select the **home** graphic, convert it to a button, and name it **HomeButton**. Add the Go To First Page action. Choose the Rollover state and use Object Layer Options to choose the **OVER** layer comp. Save the file and keep it open.

5. Now you'll delete unnecessary buttons. Double-click the page 1 thumbnail in the Pages panel to target it. Because the buttons are master page items, they are locked. Choose Override All Master Page Items from the Pages panel menu to unlock the frames containing the button artwork. Select and delete the **PrevPage** and **HomeButton** frames. Move the **NextPage** frame to the right so it's closer to the edge of the page.

6. Go to page 7. Here, you'll use a different method of unlocking the buttons, since you only want to delete the **NextPage** button and don't want to risk

messing up the arrangement of the remaining buttons. Hold down Command-Shift (Mac) or Ctrl-Shift (Windows) and click the **NextPage** button to unlock only that master item. Once it's unlocked, delete it.

7. Set the Preview panel to Preview Document mode ( ), click the Play button ( ), and test the buttons and hyperlinks. Fix any malfunctioning controls, save the file, and keep it open.

As you've seen throughout this book, adding interactive content and navigation controls can be a time-consuming endeavor. In essence, you're working hard so the viewer doesn't have to think about how to navigate through your document. I hope your client appreciates all the hard work you're doing.

Animating a Headline

Just for good measure, don't you think this magazine could use some flying text? I thought so.

1. Go to page 7 of the magazine. With the Pen tool or Pencil tool, draw a curving shape starting in the pasteboard at the lower left of the page, and ending in the center of the word **Environment**. The stroke attribute of the path is not important; once it's converted to a motion path it will lose any fill and stroke attributes and become invisible. The smoother the path, the more smoothly the word will fly in (**Figure 9.28**). Think of the path as a sort of track that the word will follow.

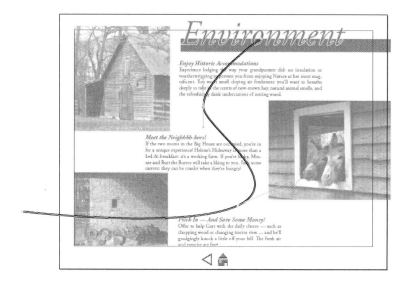

Figure 9.28 Draw a swooping path with the Pen or Pencil tool from the lower left to the center of the word **Environment**. Start several inches outside the left edge of the page.

2. Open the Animation panel (Window > Interactive > Animation). Select the text frame containing the word **Environment,** and Shift-click to select the path you drew. At the bottom of the Animation panel, click the Convert to Motion Path icon ( ). If necessary, click the triangle to the left of the Properties label in the Animation panel to reveal the Properties options. Choose the following settings, and leave other options at the defaults.

- **Event:** On Page Load

- **Duration:** 1.5 seconds

- **Speed:** Ease in

- **Animate:** To Current Location

- **Opacity:** Fade In

3. Test the flying text. You can edit the path by selecting the text frame and then switching to the Direct Selection tool and clicking the motion path to select it. You can then move points and manipulate direction handles as you can on any other path. Save the file and keep it open.

Adding a Video

To give the viewers an idea of what they're missing if they don't visit Helene's Holistic Hideaway, you'll add a video showing fun-loving raccoons playing in a giant exercise wheel. The movie was originally an AVI file from a digital camera. It was converted to the F4V format with Adobe Media Encoder.

1. Go to page 6 of the magazine. Choose File > Place, navigate to the **Ch_9_Exercises** > **Video** folder, select **raccoons.f4v**, and click Open. Click (don't drag) somewhere in the text frame to the left of the peacock photo. You may have to wait a couple of seconds for the video preview to appear.

2. Open the Media panel (Window > Interactive > Media). *Uncheck* Play on Page Load; you'll trigger the movie with a button. Set the Poster option to None, and choose the SkinOverAllNoFullNoCaption controller. (Yes, that's its name. Whew.) Check the Show Controller on Rollover option. If necessary, reposition the movie frame so it's centered over the text frame.

3. The button art has been provided as an InDesign snippet. Choose File > Place, navigate to the **Ch_9_Exercises** > **Video** folder, select **VideoButton.idms,** and click Open. Click above the peacock photo to

create the embossed text frame that will become a button; right now it's just a text frame. Position the frame so its right edge aligns with the right edge of the peacock photo.

4. Convert the text frame to a button named **playmovie**, and add the Video action. Because there's only one video in the page, the **raccoons.f4v** video is automatically designated as the target.

5. Click the Rollover state in the Buttons panel. Right-click (Mac: Control-click) and choose Effects > Drop Shadow. Add a 50% black drop shadow, with an X and Y offset of 0.07 inch (**Figure 9.29**). Set the size of the shadow to 0.07 inch, and click OK.

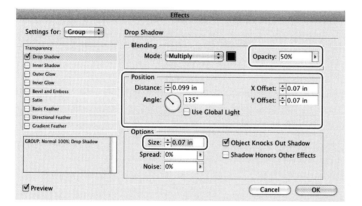

Figure 9.29 Add a drop shadow to the Rollover state of the button that will trigger the raccoon video, just to provide a bit of visual feedback to the viewer.

6. Test the spread in the Preview panel. Make sure the button triggers the video (there's no audio accompanying the playful raccoons, so you can turn your sound down now). Save the file. In the next section, you'll be working in Illustrator and Flash Professional, so you can close InDesign if you like, and take a break before you start the next part of the project.

Using Illustrator and Flash Professional

Illustrator and Flash Professional have a close relationship. Flash understands the native Illustrator format; you can import Illustrator files with control over which layers are visible, and even copy/paste directly between the applications. In this part of the lesson, you'll modify an Illustrator file, then paste its contents into a Flash document and animate it so it will fly gently. You'll export the animation to a SWF, which you'll then place in InDesign so it can fly across the page.

Modifying the Illustrator Artwork

You'll give yourself a bit of a head start by converting the Helene's Hideaway logo to a movie clip symbol before you bring it into Flash Professional.

1. Launch Adobe Illustrator. Navigate to the **Ch_9_Exercises** > **InDesign Rework** > **Links** folder, and open **helene_logo2.ai**. Select all the artwork on the artboard, and group it together (Object > Group). You don't have to group the artwork, but it does prevent wandering.

2. You need to convert the grouped artwork to a symbol. Open the Symbols panel (Window > Symbols), and drag the selected grouped artwork onto an empty area of the Symbols panel. In the Symbol Options dialog (**Figure 9.30**), name the symbol **Helene_Symbol**, accept the default settings, and click OK. This creates a new symbol and—more importantly—converts the original artwork into an instance of the symbol. Note that the default symbol type is Movie Clip; this will come in handy in Flash.

Figure 9.30 Converting the artwork to a symbol in Illustrator saves you a step in Flash Professional. You can also designate Illustrator art as a symbol during the import to Flash Professional.

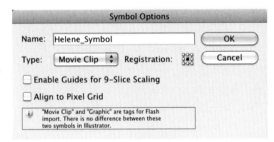

3. If necessary, reselect the logo artwork, and then copy it to the Clipboard. You don't have to change the document color mode of the Illustrator file, because its mode will become RGB when it's imported into Flash Professional.

4. Launch Flash Professional. Choose File > New to start a new document. In the dialog that appears, ActionScript 3.0 (the first option in the list of general options) should be selected. If not, select ActionScript 3.0 and click OK. The white rectangle that appears is the stage, analogous to a page in InDesign. Save the file as **FlyingLogo.fla** in the **Ch_9_Exercises** > **Illustrator to Flash** folder.

5. To ensure that the animation will fall where you intend in the final project, change the document dimensions to match the 800 px by 600 px size of the InDesign document. Choose Modify > Document and change the Width and Height values. Alternatively, you can click the Edit button by the size values in the Properties Inspector at the right side of the stage.

6. Paste the Helene's Hideaway logo artwork that's been waiting patiently on the Clipboard. If you have copied something else to the Clipboard since then, you'll probably receive an error when you attempt to paste it into the Flash document. Go back to Illustrator and recopy the artwork if necessary. Accept the default pasting options (**Figure 9.31**) and click OK.

Figure 9.31 The default options work for most situations when you paste Illustrator artwork into a Flash Professional project.

7. To help you position the flying logo correctly, choose View > Rulers if the rulers are not already visible. Zoom in on the top left corner of the stage by holding down Command-spacebar (Mac) or Ctrl-spacebar (Windows) and dragging a zoom marquee across the upper-left corner of the stage. Position your cursor in the horizontal ruler across the top of the stage, and drag down until you reach the 20 pixel mark. Then choose View > Magnification > Fit in Window.

8. Using the Selection tool at the right side of the Flash interface (like the Selection tools in other Adobe applications, it's a black arrow), move the logo movie clip to just inside the left edge of the stage, with its top edge aligned to the guide you created.

9. At the bottom of the Flash Professional interface, click the Timeline tab to show the timeline controls if they're not already visible. Go to frame 120 of the timeline, click in the small rectangle underneath the 120 mark, and choose Insert > Timeline > Frame. Alternatively, you can right-click (Mac: Control-click) in the frame rectangle and choose Insert Frame.

NOTE: The default frames-per-second rate (think of movie frames) is 24 fps in both In-Design and Flash Professional. This is a 5-second animation; $5 \times 24 = 120$.

10. Return to frame 1 of the timeline by clicking in the frame rectangle at the beginning of the timeline. Select the logo movie clip in the stage. (It may be hard to think of a stationary object as a movie clip, but this is how Flash regards it. Just go along with it.) Choose **Insert > Motion Tween**.

11. Click the Motion Tween tab, which is tucked in behind the Timeline tab. Scroll down until you see the Transformation section of the Motion Tween controls. Locate the Scale X and Scale Y controls (**Figure 9.32**). Click the blue 100% by the Scale X label, and change the value to 30%; the Scale Y value should also change, since the X and Y values are linked together.

Figure 9.32 In the first frame of the timeline, change the Scale X and Y values to 30% (initially, you'll see 100%, as shown).

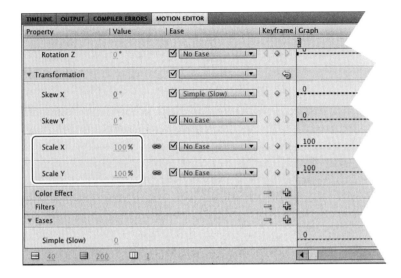

12. Now you'll add an effect to make the logo fade in as it moves across the stage. Scroll a bit farther down in the Motion Editor controls, until you see Color Effect. Click the plus sign to the right of the Color Effect entry in the list of controls, and choose Alpha from the pull-down menu that appears (**Figure 9.33**). A new row, Alpha amount, appears. Click the initial 100% value and change it to 0% (you can also scrub to the left on the value itself to reduce it to 0). You can also add and modify the Color Effect option in the Properties Inspector.

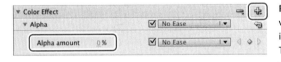

Figure 9.33 Set the Alpha value to 0% under Color Effect in the Motion Editor controls. This will initially hide the logo, so it can fade in as it moves across the page.

13. Click the Timeline tab to bring the timeline controls to the front again. Click in the last small frame rectangle, under the 120 mark. Select the logo on the stage (it will still think it's at 0% alpha, and thus invisible, but you should be able to find its bounding box; click and drag if necessary to throw a net over it). Move the bounding box of the invisible logo to the right side of the stage.

TIP: Since motion presets (including any custom motion paths) are stored as XML, they can be shared between InDesign and Flash Professional.

14. Return to the Motion Editor by clicking its tab. Scroll down to the Transformation section, and change the size to 60% for both X and Y values. In the Color Effects section, change the alpha to 100%. Now that you can actually see the logo, reposition it so it falls just inside the top and right edges of the stage.

15. Preview the animation by pressing Ctrl-Enter (Windows) or Command-Return (Mac). The logo should move sedately across the stage, becoming fully visible when it reaches the right side. Don't worry that the animation loops over and over; you'll fix that in a later step. Close the preview, save the file, and keep it open.

16. Notice the red line connecting the initial state of the logo with the current state and position of the logo. That's a visual representation of the motion tween path—and it's editable (the path is red because that's the key color of the layer it's in). With the Selection tool, click in the middle of the motion tween path and drag it downward (**Figure 9.34**). If the entire line moves, rather than being reshaped, undo and reselect the line, making sure you see a little curly icon by your cursor to indicate that you can modify the shape of the motion path.

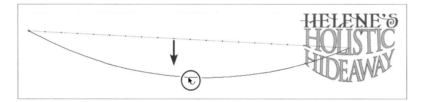

Figure 9.34 The motion path is completely editable. Just drag the nodes on the line, as you would do in Illustrator.

17. Click the Timeline tab to return to the timeline controls. Click in the small frame rectangle at the 48 marker. You'll see the position and alpha state of the logo at that moment in time. Select the logo movie clip and move it up until its top edge aligns roughly with the guideline. Notice that the motion tween path gently curves in and out of that position to provide a smooth motion (**Figure 9.35**). Preview the animation again to see the results of this move.

Figure 9.35 At frame 48, move the logo movie clip up to add another little bounce to the motion path.

18. Now you'll modify the motion tween so the animation starts out fast, then slows down as the logo lands in its final location. Click the motion path to select it. In the Properties panel on the right, enter **75** in the Ease setting. Preview the animation to see how this changes the behavior of the flying logo. Close the preview and save the file.

TIP: The gray text you see in code display is explanatory commenting provided by Flash. As you explore Flash Professional more deeply, you'll find code commenting helpful and educational.

19. Now you'll enter a Stop command, to prevent the flying logo from looping and driving your viewers mad. In the timeline, click in the last frame, under the 120 mark. Select the logo movie clip on the stage. Open the **Code Snippets** panel (Window > Code Snippets). Click the triangle to the left of Timeline Navigation in the Code Snippets panel to reveal the options under that topic (**Figure 9.36**). Double-click the Stop at this Frame command. Flash Professional creates a new layer in the timeline to hold the assigned action, and adds the code to the last frame in the timeline. The Actions-Frame panel automatically appears, showing you the code that has been added. Close the Actions-Frame panel and save the file.

Figure 9.36 When you add a Stop command in the last frame of the animation to prevent it from looping, Flash Professional displays the complete commented code in case you'd like to examine or edit it.

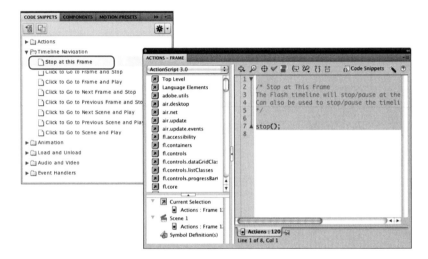

20. Now it's time to export the animation to SWF, so it can be placed in InDesign. Choose File > Publish Settings. In the Type options, uncheck everything but Flash (.swf), and click the small folder icon to the right of the filename field to choose a location for the SWF. Save the SWF as **FlyingLogo.swf** in the **Ch_9_Exercises** > **Illustrator to Flash** folder.

21. Now that you've finished animating the Illustrator logo, you can close Flash Professional. In the next section, you'll import the SWF file into the magazine project in InDesign.

Importing Flash Animation into InDesign

To finish the interactive magazine project and try to drum up business for Helene's Holistic Hideaway, you'll import the animated logo you created in the previous section.

1. Launch InDesign. Choose File > Open, navigate to the **InDesign Rework** folder, and open **MagForWebNew.indd**. Go to page 5 of the magazine. Select and delete the Helene's Holistic Hideaway logo; you'll replace the static logo with the flying version.

2. In the Layers panel, target the **buttons** layer. Choose File > Place, navigate to the **Ch_9_Exercises** > **Illustrator to Flash** folder, select **FlyingLogo.swf**, and click **Open**. Click near the upper-left corner of the page to place the animation. Since the animation was built to the same dimensions as the magazine pages, you can snap the upper-left corner of the animation to the upper-left corner of the page and it should fit perfectly.

3. In the Media panel, select the Play on Page Load option and set the Poster option to None. The animation won't be visible until the viewer lands on page 5. Then, the logo should fly in automatically and land gracefully in the position originally occupied by the static Illustrator artwork. If that doesn't drum up business for the resort, I don't know what will.

4. Perform one final check of all the interactive elements in the Preview panel. Don't forget all the hyperlinks, the navigation buttons, the slideshow, and the flying text. Once you're certain that everything is functioning as expected, choose File > Save As and overwrite the current **MagForWebNew.indd** file. Why Save As, rather than just File > Save? Every time you save an InDesign file, new information is appended to the existing file, and file size can begin to bloat. Save As rewrites the file, economizing it. This can reduce the file size, sometimes dramatically. Just for grins, note the before-and-after file size to see the difference. For example, I just performed a Save As on this chapter, and the file size went from 9.2 MB to 7.4 MB.

Exporting the Finished Project

At long last! It's time to export the magazine project to SWF and prepare the project for uploading to a Web site. You probably remember the approach from Chapter 6, but here's a short refresher course.

1. Choose File > Export, and select Flash Player (SWF) for the format. Navigate to the **Ch_9_Exercises** >**Final Project** folder, name the file **FinalMag.swf**, and click Save. In the Export SWF dialog, make sure Interactive Page Curl is deselected.

2. Your default browser should launch and display the exported SWF. Navigate through the magazine project and test all the interactive features. When you're finished, close InDesign, Flash Professional, Photoshop, Illustrator, your Web browser, your e-mail program, and anything else that's running, and take a break. You deserve it!

Checklist

When you're absorbed in a project—whether print or interactive—it's easy to develop tunnel vision, especially when you're nearly finished. Deadlines can blur your vision, so you should consider making a list that you use to check your project before you consider it finalized. It's even better if you can arrange to have someone test the finished interactive piece to see if they encounter any issues. Innocent bystanders can be invaluable.

You'll develop your own checklist over time, but here's a starter list.

Page dimensions

- Does the project fit on a typical monitor or laptop screen?

- Would the viewer need to scroll to view important content if the project was viewed on a small laptop?

Hyperlinks

- Do all the intra-document hyperlinks work correctly? Check hyperlinks to page anchors, hyperlinks to text anchors, cross-references, jumpline hyperlinks, and Table of Contents hyperlinks.

- Are hyperlinks obviously clickable?

Web links

- Are all Web links clickable?

- Are there any incorrect links (dead URLs, incorrect sites, less-than-tasteful sites as the result of a typo)?

- Are links obvious? Will the viewer know to click?

- Is it easy to hit intended links, without accidentally clicking on the wrong one in a tight space?

Navigation controls

- Are navigation buttons intuitive?

- Is it obvious which is a next or previous page button?

- Does a home button lead to the appropriate target (a cover or Table of Contents)?

- Should you include a "how the controls work" page at the beginning of the document to make sure the viewer understands the navigation?

Page transitions

- Do page transitions enhance or detract from the experience?

- Will page transitions interfere with navigation controls?

Video

- Is it obvious that there is video content? Provide a button or caption that invites the viewer to click. Otherwise, they may mistake the video for a still photograph if the video is not set to play on page load.

- Have you included a player skin so the viewer can control playback?

Audio

- Is there an obvious indicator that the viewer should click to play audio, if it's not set to play on page load?

- Is the audio long enough to be worth hearing, but not so long that it outlasts the page view?

Animations

- Is the timing correct for all animations? Do they play in the correct order?
- Do the animations play on page load, or do you need to lead the viewer to click a trigger?

Multistate objects

- Is the current state the one you want viewers to see initially?
- Have you provided controls for cycling through the states of the object?

Buttons

- Do buttons convey what they do?
- Do rollover and click appearances work?

Deployment

- Do you need to rename the host HTML file "index.html" or "default.html" for it to work properly on your Web server?

Wrapping Up

Now that you've taken this trip through InDesign, Photoshop, Illustrator, and Flash Professional, you should have a much better idea how to tackle your next interactive project. You should be comfortable with the new interactive features in InDesign CS5, and perhaps inspired to move outside your print-centric comfort zone.

Welcome to the future. Now go have fun with your new toys!

Index

Meet Creative Edge.

A new resource of unlimited books, videos and tutorials for creatives from the world's leading experts.

Creative Edge is your one stop for inspiration, answers to technical questions and ways to stay at the top of your game so you can focus on what you do best—being creative.

All for only $24.99 per month for access—any day any time you need it.

creative
edge

R.C.L.

AVR. 2011

G

peachpit.com/creativeedge